"If I was going to undertake the challenge of developing and maintaining a truly effective business contingency program, I can't imagine a more practical and useful guide than Michael's Scrappy BCP book."
Jack Jones, Founder and President of Risk Management Insight

"Scrappy BCP gets right down to business in helping the reader create a comprehensive continuity plan for their company, large or small."
Lisa Orloff, Founder and Executive Director, World Cares Center

"I really liked it! The majority of books/articles are rather dry. This was compelling with some light humor. It certainly kept my attention and kept me reading!"
Cheyene Haase, President, BC Management, Inc.

"Every successful business manager, regardless of the size of the business or what stage it is in, needs to read Scrappy Business Contingency Planning. After all, disasters matter only to successful businesses; if your business is already a disaster, you don't need to worry about planning for one."
Will Luden, Past CEO of InfoPartners (purchased by Compushare)

Scrappy Business Contingency Planning

How to Bullet-Proof Your Business and Laugh at Volcanoes, Tornadoes, Locust Plagues, and Hard Drive Crashes

By Michael Seese

A Happy About® series
20660 Stevens Creek Blvd., Suite 210,
Cupertino, CA 95014

Published by Scrappy About™, a Happy About® series
20660 Stevens Creek Blvd., Suite 210, Cupertino, CA 95014
http://scrappyabout.com

First Printing: November 2010
Paperback ISBN: 978-1-60005-150-0 (1-60005-150-2)
eBook ISBN: 978-1-60005-151-7 (1-60005-151-0)
Place of Publication: Silicon Valley, California, USA
Paperback Library of Congress Number: 2010939038

Trademarks

Warning and Disclaimer

Author's Note

Scrappy Business Contingency Planning is a battery-powered emergency light in an otherwise dark and scary world...that of the unknown.

What would happen to us if we couldn't get into our office for end-of-quarter processing?

I don't know.

What would happen to us if we lost our internet connection for a week?

I don't know.

What would happen to us if the CEO dies?

I don't know.

What else don't we know?

I don't know.

Our reliance on technology, competition from abroad, and the whims of nature make this an increasingly scary time to be in business. You don't need a tidal wave to submerge your enterprise; a power surge in the data center could do the job just fine, thank you.

Scrappy Business Contingency Planning offers a step-by-step guide to establishing a business contingency (BC) program from the ground up—or from the sky down—taking you from 50,000-foot planning to 100-foot planning to an inch-above-the-ground, nitty-gritty detailed planning. Those without a program can follow the steps detailed in the book from cover to cover. But even those whose organization has an established BC program will find tips, pitfalls, and other nuggets of information that possibly no one had thought of.

Scrappy Business Contingency Planning. So that you never have to say, "I don't know."

Meet the Scrappy Guides™

The Scrappy Guides™ are books to help you be unrealistic and accomplish what seems impossible, but is merely difficult. Those of you who say it can't be done should stay out of the way of those of us doing it!

Scrappy means ATTITUDE.

Scrappy means not relying on a title to be a leader.

Scrappy means being willing to take risks and put yourself out there.

Scrappy means doing the right thing, even when you don't feel like it.

Scrappy means having the steely resolve of a street fighter.

Scrappy means sticking to your guns even if you're shaking in your boots.

Scrappy means being committed beyond reason to making a difference.

Scrappy means caring about something more than you care about being comfortable, socially acceptable, or politically correct.

Scrappy means being absolutely, totally committed to extraordinary results.

Scrappy means EDGY!...and is your edge in achieving outrageous results even when they seem impossible.

The Scrappy Guides™ help you muster the courage and commitment to pursue your goals—even when there is no evidence that you can succeed—yet! They are your shield against the naysayers who will try to undermine you, and they will give you comfort during the inevitable setbacks that accompany most worthy pursuits. When you fail, fail fast, fail forward, in the direction of your goals, lurching fitfully if you must. Sometimes success is built on the foundation of a very tall junk pile.

Let's get Scrappy!

The Books in the Scrappy Guides™ Series

Kimberly Wiefling
Scrappy Project Management: *The 12 Predictable and Avoidable Pitfalls Every Project Faces*

Julie Abrams, Carole Amos, Eldette Davie, Mai-Huong Le, Hannah Kain, Sue Lebeck, Terrie Mui, Pat Obuchowski, Yuko Shibata, Nathalie Udo, Betty Jo Waxman, Kimberly Wiefling
Scrappy Women in Business: *Living Proof That Bending the Rules Isn't Breaking the Law*

Michael Seese
Scrappy Information Security: *The Easy Way to Keep the Cyber Wolves at Bay*
Scrappy Business Contingency Planning: *How to Bullet-Proof Your Business and Laugh at Volcanoes, Tornadoes, Locust Plagues, and Hard Drive Crashes*

Michael Horton
Scrappy General Management: *Common Sense Practices to Avoid Calamities, Catastrophes, and Lackluster Results for Corporations and Small Businesses*

Meet the Scrappy Guides™ Executive Editor

Hi, I'm Kimberly Wiefling, Founder and President of my own consulting business, Wiefling Consulting, Executive Editor of the Scrappy Guides™, and the Author of *Scrappy Project Management: The 12 Predictable and Avoidable Pitfalls Every Project Faces*, growing in popularity around the world and published in Japanese by Nikkei Business Press. The biggest compliment that anyone has ever paid me is that I am a "force of nature." Actually, I'm not sure they meant it in a positive way—they certainly could have been referring to destructive forces like hurricanes, tsunamis, earthquakes, and the like. Nevertheless, Mother Nature is one of my favorite gal pals, and I'm pleased to be associated with her in this way.

My dad was a welder, my brothers were both welders, and, if I had been born a boy, I probably would have been a welder, too! But, as luck would have it, I grew up in a time when girls weren't encouraged to be welders. So I went to college instead, earning a B.S. in chemistry and physics and an M.S. in physics. But don't be so quick to write me off, 'cause I've got marketable skills, too! For example, I earned a marksman's ribbon while in the U.S. Air Force right after high school (I used my GI Bill money to pay for college), where I learned to repair electronics equipment. And I spent ten years working at HP in various engineering and technical jobs, including one that involved a long stretch of explosion testing and other destructive testing of lovingly handcrafted one-of-a-kind R&D prototypes. (My motto was, "When it absolutely, positively has to be destroyed overnight—bring it to me!") I got bored with all of the stability and job security of HP, so I quit and joined a series of failed startups (not all my fault!) and then started my own consulting company during the dot-com bust of 2001—not exactly the most hospitable environment in which to launch a business. I lurched fitfully forward for three long years before my big break came—a chance to work in Japan with my Japanese "sister" Yuko Shibata of ALC Education, Inc., starting up their Global Management Consulting Group.

In typical Silicon Valley style, I've helped to start, run, and grow about a dozen small businesses, some of which are still in business and profitable. My clients include Cisco Systems, Symantec, Intuit, HP, Agilent Technologies, Mazda, Daiichi Sankyo, Dow Corning Toray, Mitsubishi Heavy Industries, the University of California, Siemens, Hitachi, Alcoa, Xerox PARC, NECsoft, NTT DoCoMo, and many more.

Now I do more than half of my consulting work in Japan, traveling there every month with a team of people who deliver intensive workshops that enable participants to achieve what seems impossible but is merely difficult. (That's my specialty!) These global leaders emerge from these programs with new eyes to see the opportunities in which we are all swimming, a global mindset, and the determination to solve global problems profitably—for their companies and for the sake of all the people of the world. It's like a dream come true for me, and my experiences have ranged from hilarious to deeply moving.

In pursuit of planetary transformation, I'm contributing to making the world a better place in a number of ways. I'm the Co-founder of the Open Kilowatt Institute (OKI) and the Founding Co-chair of the SDForum Engineering Leadership Special Interest Group (EL SIG). I'm supporting micro-finance for entrepreneurs throughout the world via Kiva, and I support the economic independence of women in various ways because I believe that this is the most effective way to raise the quality of life for all people.

I am obsessed with collaboration, and you can reach me via email at kimberly@wiefling.com.

Become a Scrappy Guides™ Author

Have a "Scrappy" streak in you? Want to write about it? Contact me and let's talk! Email me at kimberly@wiefling.com.

Dedication

To all the people who have, knowingly or unknowingly, willfully or accidentally, gracefully or maliciously, mentored me in the art and practice and folly of life.

Acknowledgments

I would like to thank my beautiful wife, Jean, who supports me in so many ways, and who tolerated the many nights she shared me with a laptop;

...My precious children, who have no such tolerance for sharing;

...Izzie, who (sadly) never worried about a hard drive crash;

...My Mom and Dad, without whom I wouldn't be possible;

...the rest of my family and friends;

...Chuck Caputo, who has been a friend and a mentor; much of the wisdom in this book I learned from him;

...Pete Nofel, who offered me the "buddy rate" for his editing services. (And we're still friends.);

...Steven Crimando and Marv Wainschel, who reviewed a draft and offered me some real, usable, constructive comments; and

...Kimberly, who has said many wacky things to me over the years, most recently, "Why don't you write another book?"

A Message from Happy About®

Thank you for your purchase of this Scrappy About book, a series from Happy About®. It is available online at: http://www.happyabout.com/scrappyabout/scrappy-bcp.php or at other online and physical bookstores.

- Please contact us for quantity discounts at sales@happyabout.info.
- If you want to be informed by email of upcoming Happy About® books, please email bookupdate@happyabout.info.

Happy About is interested in you if you are an author who would like to submit a non-fiction book proposal or a corporation that would like to have a book written for you. Please contact us by email at editorial@happyabout.info or phone (1-408-257-3000).

Other Happy About books available include:

- Scrappy Project Management®: http://happyabout.info/scrappyabout/project-management.php
- Scrappy Women in Business: http://bit.ly/scrappybizwomen[1]
- Scrappy General Management: http://bit.ly/scrappygm [2]
- Scrappy Information Security: http://www.happyabout.com/scrappyabout/scrappy-infosec.php
- #PROJECT MANAGEMENT tweet Book01: http://happyabout.com/thinkaha/projectmanagementtweet01.php
- The Ten Commandments for Effective Standards: http://bit.ly/10ceffectivestds[3]
- #LEADERSHIPtweet Book01: http://www.happyabout.com/thinkaha/leadershiptweet01.php
- The Successful Introvert: http://www.happyabout.com/thesuccessfulintrovert.php
- Expert Product Management: http://www.happyabout.com/expertproductmanagement.php
- Agile Excellence for Product Managers: http://www.happyabout.com/agileproductmangers.php
- #QUALITYtweet Book01: http://www.happyabout.com/thinkaha/qualitytweet01.php

1. www.happyabout.com/scrappyabout/scrappywomeninbusiness.php
2. www.happyabout.com/scrappyabout/scrappy-general-management.php
3. www.happyabout.com/synopsyspress/10commandmentseffective standards.php

Contents

Contents

Graphics

Preface

> "One of the true tests of leadership is the ability to recognize a problem before it becomes an emergency."
> *- Arnold H. Glasgow*

When I first heard about the field of business contingency planning—BCP—I said to my wife, "This is the perfect career for me. It's an opportunity to put my obsessive-compulsive disorder to good use." I was joking, of course. But there was a kernel of truth to my quip. Business contingency planning (BCP) is about thinking of everything that could go wrong, and then developing a planned response just in case it actually happens. Only someone blessed (or cursed) with a mind that churns will think through the details and ramifications of every possibility. As an example, you might think that placing your contingency plans on employees' laptop computers would eliminate the need for printed copies. But what if the disaster *du jour* is a widespread power outage, and there is no electricity for printers? Would you really expect your employees to memorize or hand-write documents that could range from 50 pages or more? Probably not. Or maybe they could just carry around their laptops as they race to execute the plans before the batteries die. At least the light from the computer screen would make up for a lack of flashlights.

This example illustrates the power of negative thinking. Only someone who worries too much would think of that one!

Most of us have jobs with a varying degree of what I call the "drone" factor: you go to work, sit at a desk, and type type type or file file file so that you can make the corporation money. Bear in mind, there is nothing wrong with that. But if you are involved in your organization's contingency planning efforts, you are doing a great deal more. You are helping to ensure the viability of your employer in the face of a catastrophic event. It is not an exaggeration to say that a disaster could drive the guy across the street—who failed to plan—out of business. But your employer—having a solid BCP program—will live, allowing you to type type type or file file file (thereby getting paid paid paid) another day.

I'll stress throughout this book that BCP is about *planning*. I personally think that many of us could benefit from a refresher course on good planning principles as we prepare our home disaster kits, or even as we book our next vacation.

Each of us faces countless problems and inconveniences—most of them minor, of course—on a daily basis. As you deal with your daily disasters, keep in mind what I like to think of as one of the central tenets of planning, period:

Focus on the loss, not the event!

Consider all of the things that could go wrong as you try to race to work on time:

- You could run out of gas.

- You could get a flat tire.

- You could get caught in traffic.

- You could get stuck at a railroad crossing.

- You could...

Well, actually, you could go crazy just trying to come up with an all-inclusive list. So instead of worrying about the thousand "ifs," focus on the loss—in this case, your loss of a timely arrival—and how to deal with that.

Read on and learn how to cope...

Kick Off

"Expect the best, plan for the worst, and prepare to be surprised."
- Denis Waitley

I first got the idea to write this book while on a business and pleasure trip to San Francisco. Returning to the hotel after the first day of the conference, my wife lamented our lack of an internet-connected computer, which would have eased the task of finding sources of entertainment for our active two-year-old. Fortunately, we were able to fall back on more prehistoric methods: we talked with some local folks, and we used the telephone. OK, I'll admit that I also called a friend and asked him to search the web to glean some information for us.

The approach I used to find sources of amusement for our toddler is one of the tenets of contingency planning. If you think hard enough, you will find one or more alternatives to whatever is puzzling you. Each alternative presents its own challenges, and typically is less efficient than your normal routine. That's why they're called "backup" plans, rather than standard operating procedures. But they do the job. And sometimes the alternatives suggest a whole new way of doing things in your normal process.

The technique of stepping back and considering how things were done in the past, so-called "retro" processes, is often overlooked while contemplating solutions. When trying to think of strategies to keep a business running in a time of crisis, you may find the answer by recalling how you used to get things done in the "Dark Ages," before Al Gore invented the Internet. After all, commerce did take place before email, faxes, and telephones. It may not have been as efficient or productive, but it happened. Of course, not every business can roll back the clock. An automated manufacturing firm would be hard-pressed to put a wrench in a worker's hand and say, "Have at it!" But, many organizations could limp along temporarily using 20th century methods until the power comes back on. The moral of the story? When developing your contingency plans, focus on the technology-based alternates, but don't overlook the manual ones. Consider that NASA developed a fancy ink pen that could write reliably in zero gravity, while the Soviets got by just fine using a pencil.

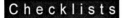

Scrappy BCP Checklists

Although later in the book I somewhat "pooh-pooh" the idea of simply checking items off a to-do list, the fact is that there are certain steps which must be followed when developing a business contingency program and plans. Below are two lists which you can use for handy reference.

Business Contingency Program Steps

☐ Identify Assets

☐ Rate System/Application/Data Criticality

☐ Determine System/Application/
Data Recovery Order

☐ Determine the "Pain" Threshold

☐ Determine Existing Vulnerabilities

☐ Examine Potential Threats

☐ Evaluate Countermeasures

☐ Review Audits

☐ Focus on the Loss, Not the Event

☐ Research and Establish Backup Storage Alternatives

☐ Research and Establish Recovery Alternatives

☐ Establish Lines of Succession

- ☐ Establish Disaster Criteria

- ☐ Establish Disaster Declaration Criteria

- ☐ Establish Relationships with Local Emergency Services

- ☐ Develop Communications Plans

- ☐ Establish Business Contingency Plan Distribution Strategy

- ☐ Establish Return-to-Normal Criteria

Business Contingency Plan Steps

- ☐ Catalog Personnel Information

- ☐ Catalog Job Functions

- ☐ Catalog Business Processes

- ☐ Draft Detailed Standard Operating Procedures

- ☐ Catalog Equipment Requirements

- ☐ Develop Manual Procedures

- ☐ Establish Call Trees

- ☐ Cross-Train Job Functions

1 What Is BCP?

"What, me worry?"
- Alfred E. Neuman

Any business, be it a manufacturer or a service provider, sells its customers what they think they want and need. The bold ones—innovators or just plucky hopefuls—create something new, and then convince us that we can't live without it. Technology does the same thing for corporations. Twenty years ago, no one had heard of BCP. Today, no sensible business dares to live without it.

But, what is BCP? A colleague and I discussed what we should call this profession of ours, this business of thinking about and preparing for "bad things." Although BCP is commonly known as business *continuity* planning, that "de-acronym," we agreed, focuses too much on continuing—on "business as usual"—in the face of disruption and disaster. Instead, we felt that business *contingency* planning captures the spirit of the profession much more completely.

When presenting a "BCP Basics" seminar, I always ask the audience, "What is BCP?" After hearing their fast and furious (OK, usually slow and grudging) answers, I offer mine:

- Risk analysis
- Emergency response
- Event evaluation
- Business relocation
- Business resumption
- Continuity of operations
- Restoration and recovery
- "Return to normal," bearing in mind that the new normal might seem rather abnormal at first

As you can see, continuing operations is only a small part of the effort, and fails to take into account many of the absolutely critical steps outlined above, such as evaluating the situation, reviewing alternatives, restoring operations, and returning to normal. But if you call it business *contingency* planning, you are planning for any contingency, small or large, mundane or sensational.

The bottom line is that you are trying to prepare your organization to withstand an unlikely, though not unpredictable or unexpected, event—something that "can't happen here." A *really good* business contingency plan will help you not only weather an event that can't happen here, but even continue to delight your customers and make a profit.

2 The Power of Negative Thinking

"Accidents will happen
We only hit and run."
- *Declan Patrick MacManus a.k.a. Elvis Costello*

Aside from the terrible human loss, the terrorist attacks of 9/11 served as a horrifying reminder that an unimaginable event can cause unimaginable repercussions. The destruction of the World Trade Center meant that businesses based there lost their physical center of operations as well as the unfortunate people who died there. But the ripple effect extended far beyond the enterprises housed in the towers.

The buildings' collapse damaged a telephone-switching station in Lower Manhattan and disrupted communications throughout the city. The Port Authority Trans-Hudsonline (PATH) subway station below the World Trade Center was completely destroyed. Before the attacks, about 67,000 riders passed through the station daily.[4] Almost 600 feet of the tunnel surrounding subway lines 1 and 9 caved in, and the damage was so severe that more than 6,000 feet of line required complete reconstruction.[5]

But on September 10 I doubt anyone gave even the remotest thought to what would happen if it all came crashing down.

In the somber days and weeks after the attacks enterprises located in high-risk areas—major American cities like my hometown, Cleveland, for example—were suddenly scurrying about updating, or creating, plans to continue operations in the event of another attack. One of the fears was that the next strike would be a bombing—chemical, biological, or radiological—which could render a city uninhabitable. Federal funding was provided to local governments in high-risk areas to help governments and corporations prepare for events that previously had been completely unthinkable to ordinary citizens.

The upside was that the federal government's efforts benefited municipalities that were able to secure federal aid. The downside was that many local governments did not receive any federal funds. They had just as much motivation to plan, but their budgets did not have the capacity to remodel the local school, let alone fund a doom-and-gloom response program. So they opted for schools over disaster planning.

Fortunately, there have not been further attacks...yet. (What can I say; I have terrific powers of negative thinking!) Those without a planned response have continued as before, and without spending the time or money to create a BCP program. However, they probably also adopted a dangerous collective mentality. In some sense they've been rewarded for their lack of planning because nothing bad happened. But human beings are notoriously poor judges of probability. Thinking "What? Me worry?" is dangerous. Saying "It can't happen here" is dangerous. Because it can.

---

4. Moore, M. "Quiet Since 9/11, Subway To WTC Resumes Sunday." USA Today. 2003. Downloaded 11/17/2007 from
   http://www.usatoday.com/news/sept11/2003-11-19-wtc-subway_x.htm
5. Kennedy, R. "Subway At Trade Center To Take Years To Rebuild." The New York Times. 2001. Downloaded 11/17/2007 from http://bit.ly/c0Ik8B (query.nytimes.com/gst/fullpage.html?res=9805E5DE1F3AF93BA1575AC0A 9679C8B63&sec=&spon=&pagewanted=1)

Any government or corporate chieftain, or normal everyday Joe, who believes that his anonymous location in Middle Town America is not a potential terrorist target should take a look around and ask:

- Is there a chemical plant or oil refinery in the area?
- Is the facility located downstream from a dam? Destroying a dam certainly would be a daunting task, but one which would be a home run for a terrorist.
- Is there a military facility, such as a National Guard armory, nearby? If not a target, any military site could experience an accident involving munitions. Try not to think about the August 2007 snafu at Minot Air Force Base, where personnel there lost track of six nuclear missiles. Whoops! Don't worry; they were found at another air force base.[6] And people think airport baggage handlers are good at losing things.
- Are there *any* government buildings nearby? Prior to April 19, 1995, most people in Oklahoma City viewed the Alfred P. Murrah Federal Building as just another office.

This sort of analysis, leveraging the power of negative thinking, is necessary to overcome the all-too-prevalent "it can't happen here" mentality. But even if you could say that your facility has no potential targets nearby, a truly skilled negative thinker could imagine an almost infinite number of disasters—large and small, natural or manmade—that could affect your operations. Let me illustrate with another provocative question culled from one of my "BCP Basics" talks.

"We all know about 9/11, but what about 11/12/2001?" I ask

"11/12/2001? What happened on 11/12/2001?" someone in the puzzled, and otherwise silent, audience asks.

That was the day American Airlines flight 587 crashed into a Queens neighborhood shortly after takeoff, killing 260, including almost a dozen people on the ground. Although the initial investigation focused

---

6. Hoffman, M. "Nuclear Safety Slipped For Years Before Minot." Air Force Times. 2008. Downloaded 11/20/2008 from
http://www.airforcetimes.com/news/2008/02/airforce_250208_nukesafety/

on a terrorist act, authorities later determined that the crash was caused by the first officer's aggressive maneuvers in response to the turbulence coming from the wake of a nearby aircraft.[7]

The moral of this story is that planes sometimes simply fall out of the sky. (Thankfully, not often!) But these kinds of things do happen. And they *can* happen "here." If a calamitous event never happens to you, be grateful. If it does, be prepared.

---

7. Downloaded 12/29/2007 from
   http://en.wikipedia.org/wiki/American_Airlines_Flight_587

Chapter 2: The Power of Negative Thinking

3 Developing Your Business Contingency Program

"Life is what happens to you while you're busy making other plans."

- John Lennon

Developing a business contingency program from scratch is not a "quick hit" effort—something you can crank out in an afternoon and distribute in an email to the rest of your organization where it will languish in their inboxes unread. It is a major undertaking requiring senior management support, end-user buy-in, and the cooperation of representatives from every area in your organization. Anyone who has tried to build consensus on something *simple* knows that this kind of collaboration doesn't come easily!

When developing a BCP strategy, remember that contingency planning is not just an IT issue. Sure, data recovery will be at the heart of any restoration effort. As such, the IT department will play a major part in planning, maintaining, and perhaps executing the plan. But if IT is the heart, then employees are the soul, because contingency plans exist to sustain, or re-create, mission-critical tasks during unusual circumstances.

The 8 Ps

Business contingency planning involves recognizing the importance of the eight Ps: people, performance, processes, priorities, product, partners, place, and practice.

- **People:** The raw material of business operations is data. But, data alone doesn't make a business, and certainly doesn't make a profit. Data needs people to do something with it. So before an event, have people categorize and prioritize the details of their jobs. Ask them to test the contingency plans, and help update them if necessary. During a crisis, you will be asking them to overcome adversity, work under challenging and stressful conditions, do more than ever before with less, and do it well. Afterwards, you will want them to be as good as, if not better than, they were before—more experienced and better equipped to handle the next unlikely, seemingly impossible, event.

- **Performance**: In an emergency, your employees will be asked to do not only their jobs, but also those of others. And, even though they may be working outside of their core competencies, they will need to do them as best they can in order to keep the business running. An event that affects only your operations, and not your competitors, means that they will be in business and you will be struggling. Super-human performance will be necessary to prevent competitors from taking advantage of your misfortune.

- **Processes:** Whether written down or not, almost every business has standard operating procedures. In typical business environments, these processes can be modeled using SIPOC (Supplier–Input–Process–Output–Consumer). A supplier provides an input A to process B, which leads to output C, which makes its way to the consumer of that output, whether it is an external customer or another internal department. A disaster rudely interrupts the process chain. Scrappy BCP requires that you anticipate and figure out how to overcome an interruption at any point in the chain.

- **Priorities:** While a lot of stuff is important, there are a few critical things that are absolutely essential to the survival of your organization. Determine which processes these are, and make them as bulletproof as possible. You probably don't have the time or the money to address everything, but the Scrappy BCP professional is adept at getting the biggest bang for the buck. Once you've identified your priorities, determine the steps that must be taken to ensure that these processes are recovered quickly and completely. Lack of clear priorities is a problem in daily business practice, not just during a disaster. Don't expect your people to figure out priorities in the midst of a crisis. Failure to prioritize will result in the "important many" being addressed at the expense of the "critical few," just as it does in most businesses on a daily basis.

- **Product:** Your company is in the business of providing something of value, be it widgets or services. Crisis or no crisis, your customers want a steady stream of those widgets and services. Could you outsource the manufacturing of your product to another vendor, perhaps someone you already use when demand exceeds your capacity? Of course, loyal customers will understand delays, and may be patient for a while. But patience is finite, and soon they will look elsewhere to get their needs met. To keep their business, enlist them as partners before disaster strikes.

- **Partners:** BCP partnerships extend beyond traditional notions. Just like in close friendships, the time to build mutually supportive relationships and alliances is before you need them. Establish effective partnerships with suppliers, local emergency services, and even with your competitors. Believe it or not, a competitor may be willing to help, in return for reciprocity. When I was in college, I worked for a mom-and-pop pizza shop. Well, actually it was just a "pop" pizza shop, and when pop had to go to the hospital for a few days, another locally owned pizzeria stepped in and helped us out. More recently, following a 1,000-year flood in the spring of 2010, restaurant and nightclub owners in Nashville, Tennessee, banded together to help re-open those businesses which were key to attracting tourists. They knew that there wouldn't be much revenue flowing into any of their establishments without out-of-town visitors. When disaster strikes, the foundation of a more understanding and collaborative attitude will already be in place.

- **Place:** Even though business these days is being done more and more in a virtual space, many enterprises still need a physical location, at least for the server farm and a couple of human beings. Your employees spend roughly 25 percent of their lives at work (unless you are a start-up company, in which case your employees are spending about 90% of their time at work, saving on rent and living under their desks). Even in a normal company, work is a bit like a home away from home. But, that home comes with challenges. A large part of BCP is understanding the physical requirements tied to your workplace and preparing response strategies accordingly. Plan for another location that meets both your business needs and your employees' expectations.

- **Practice, Practice, Practice:** Contingency plans are not meant to be theoretical. They're not some hypothetical thought experiment. They require testing, revision, and re-testing. Consider the rigorous, repetitive training that NASA's astronauts undergo. The months and months of preparation ensure that their response to emergencies comes as second nature. Practicing a response reduces the likelihood of panic if and when that situation actually occurs. Make sure your organization gets a chance to do a proper dress rehearsal before the big show.

Remember, there are no one-size-fits-all solutions. For that reason, the tasks outlined in the following sections are guidelines, a starting place to be used for crafting customized plans appropriate to your organization.

Scope and Project Initiation

The first steps to getting your contingency plan development project rolling are:

1. Establish Planning Teams/BCP Task Force
2. Identify Scope

1. Establish Planning Teams/BCP Task Force

You probably think a Scrappy book would never advocate creating a task force, calling a bunch of meetings, and getting custom-made mugs. Well, I hate to disappoint you so early in the book, but the first step in launching a business contingency program is determining the level at which the program will operate. While bureaucratic committees and unproductive meetings are the butt of jokes in corporate America, you will need to get the key players together in a room to kick off your Scrappy BCP program. Invariably you'll need to discuss dreaded buzzwords such as "leveraging" and "synergies." Senior management, departmental representatives, and IT staffers will need to clarify goals, decide how to implement and administer the business contingency program, how much money to spend, and what the critical success factors are.

Although there is no substitute for personal involvement in building commitment to the results, smaller organizations may spare the majority of stakeholders the initial task force meetings by establishing a team of contingency planning professionals who go out and interview the subject-matter experts (SMEs) in the various lines of business. This team then uses that information to draft the initial plans, which the SMEs review, usually in their spare time, between "real" work. This team then tests, revises, and maintains the plans with the help of their departmental representatives.

For a large company, this approach is not practical. The complexity of a large business makes it difficult—if not impossible—for a small team to understand what happens daily in every single department throughout the organization. It would simply be too time-consuming for a small team to learn enough to document the minutiae and nuances of complex and granular business processes. A better strategy is to have each department nominate a contingency planning point of contact, which should be pitched to them as a "professional development opportunity." This person then is tasked with cataloging the necessary business processes and creating the plan components. In a program structured in this way, your business contingency planners serve as teachers and mentors, helping the designated points of contact determine what must be included in their plans, and then working *with* them to develop the plans.

2. Identify Scope

Another high-level consideration is the plan's scope. A smaller enterprise may develop a plan that covers the entire organization. A larger business should have separate plans for each business unit. And a geographically dispersed business should tailor its plans by region, since each area of the country may subject to different kinds of disasters. After all, there is no need to plan for tidal waves in Kansas, and the chances of snowstorms wiping out power to large chunks of the city don't need to be considered in Dubai.

Impact Analysis

"Sometimes you're the windshield, sometimes you're the bug."
- Mary-Chapin Carpenter

Once you have developed a framework for your contingency planning program by identifying the team and establishing the scope, you need to determine what to protect, what to protect it against, and how to protect it. Here are the steps critical to this part of the process:

1. Identify Assets
2. Rate System/Application/Data Criticality
3. Determine System/Application/Data Recovery Order
4. Determine the "Pain" Threshold
5. Determine Existing Vulnerabilities
6. Establish Configuration Management
7. Examine Potential Threats
8. Evaluate Countermeasures
9. Review Audits
10. Focus on the Loss, Not the Event

Chapter 3: Developing Your Business Contingency Program

BCP is like an insurance policy. Most homeowners never make use of their insurance policies to replace their homes. The same holds true for a business. Even in this uncertain world, most organizations will never use their full disaster plans, and many may never use any part of it. For that reason, people with no imagination for disaster—and already fully occupied with daily tasks—may wonder why they are spending time planning for something that seems highly unlikely to occur. Yet, just as no sensible banker would lend money for a house without insurance, no business should operate without a BC plan. (If any Fortune 500 companies out there *are* trying to squeak by without a BC plan, please let me know. I want to sell my stock immediately.) Try living through one weekend at home without electricity, heat (including hot water!) phone, or the use of your car, and you will quickly get the idea of how thin a line exists between modern society and the Stone Age.

Of utmost importance in BCP is the process of identifying assets, reviewing systems, and determining vulnerabilities, threats, and countermeasures. In short, performing risk assessments and business impact analyses.

SCRAPPY TIP: Ask people in your organization, "If a disruption were to occur today, how quickly and fully could we resume our business?" If they don't seem to think there's a need for BCP, ask them to lend you their computer and mobile phone for the rest of the day. It shouldn't take more than two hours for the symptoms of withdrawal to begin.

1. Identify Assets

To assess potential threats representatives from each department must determine which assets to protect. No company has the time or money to protect everything, so Scrappy BCPers prioritize ruthlessly, and then focus on the most important areas. Examining, listing, and establishing a financial value for company data may seem like an esoteric exercise. But it isn't.

First, cataloging your proprietary knowledge, trade secrets, and customer lists—and assigning a monetary value to them—underscores the idea that data is a valuable asset. Even in the Information Age, 20th-century minds may think of physical objects when determining which assets are most worth protecting. But physical objects are the easiest to recover. Most can be replaced by purchase, or if you're really desperate, stealing. If money can quickly replace an asset, it's not a problem; it's simply an expense. In contrast, knowledge, stored in electronic format, could be difficult or impossible, to restore without advance preparation—at any price. (And there are plenty of stories about IT departments carefully making backups only to find that they cannot restore the data after a loss.)

Second, a review of your information assets is a necessary step in determining what—and where—they are. An enterprise that has been in business for a number of years will have data in paper files, on a mainframe, on centralized servers, and—regrettably—on individual PCs and removable media. In an ideal world, your organization would identify and consolidate critical files, preferably in the cloud somewhere where it's someone else's responsibility to recover in the event of a disaster. The dream of every Scrappy BCPer is to take this mountain of unstructured but valuable data and put it someplace that allows it to be sliced, diced, analyzed—heck, even *found*—regardless of any state of emergency. Short of that Herculean effort, knowing *which* files to protect can simplify the backup process. Even more troubling than data stored at the PC level is data stored "biologically," that is, it exists *only* in someone's head, and would be unrecoverable were something to happen to that particular head. Employees quit, become critically ill, or win the lottery. Information critical to your business, but known only to them, has to be discovered, and then copied to a more reliable format. And don't underestimate the uneasiness some people may feel in realizing that your BCP efforts might make them less indispensable! (Addressing this fear will be covered in the section "The Job Security Argument," in the chapter "Selling To Employees.")

SCRAPPY TIP: Actually, most American corporations are already facing a disaster with regard to their biologically-stored information and don't even know it. The baby-boom generation—the 76 million of us born between 1946 and 1964—are reaching retirement age. (Not that we'll be able to afford to retire, mind you!) Their skills, expertise, and knowledge may soon be winging their way toward sunnier climes, leaving behind a befuddled, yet capable, workforce of "young 'uns." A proactive business should see this mass exodus coming, and find a way to match a grizzled veteran with a hungry young up-and-comer for some critical knowledge transfer before it's too late.

Third, a review of your organization's current assets might reveal that some data is not as mission-critical as first thought, and not in need of protection. Trade secrets, proprietary software programs, and HR records certainly should be guarded and backed up often. However, even trade secrets have a shelf life. As such, archiving obsolete data—or, even maintaining it—may be a waste of time, effort, and money. Beyond any legal requirements for document retention, do you really need to preserve records from the strategic planning or budgeting process from the last five years? Let's be honest: many companies don't even follow those plans after they are made anyhow! Keeping them just preserves the evidence that the whole "strategic planning retreat" was just a boondoggle.

Last, an asset review provides you with a roadmap of what must be done. Instead of a hazy understanding of possible vulnerabilities and threats, you will now have a clear focus for your BCP program. You may discover that existing safeguards protecting your organizational assets are more vulnerable than they appear. For example, current policy may mandate that databases be backed up each night. However, if the archival media are stored near the computer room, it may be protected against threats like hacking or e-theft, but still be completely vulnerable to physical threats like a fire or flood. Daily off-site storage of the media would significantly mitigate data loss, unless that off-site storage facility is in the basement of an agitated worker who suddenly goes haywire over a cheating wife or gambling debts. (It may sound funny, but it is not unheard of for backup media to go home with an employee.) So, join the 21st century. Electronic backup off-site is now easy and affordable for even small enterprises.

The proliferation of documents, spreadsheets, and email containing the first two as attachments is prompting many organizations to adopt enterprise content management systems to administer corporate information across multiple media. For some businesses, it is an effort to control "data creep," not to be confused with Richard Nixon's CREEP efforts of the last century. (If you remember this you are definitely showing your age.) Others, facing increased regulatory oversight, are using content management to help demonstrate compliance with increasingly strict privacy and security mandates. The ever-present threat of litigation has made e-discovery a reality that must be considered. Regardless of the business driver, an enterprise content management process will benefit your contingency planning efforts, because if the information is properly classified, the review process described above will be partially done.

Anyone who has personally managed a move from one computer to another knows the value of a well-organized content management system. If you have your precious files spread all over God's green acre of your hard drive, you'll be spending a great deal more time making the transition. Having all of your personal data in one place makes it much easier to electronically schlep it from point A to point B. Likewise, when your mission-critical data has been stored in a logical fashion, your recovery teams will be able to find it and restore it with less effort.

2. Rate System/Application/Data Criticality

Every organization has numerous applications and systems in use. Some may be necessary business functions, yet their short-term absence would have no negative impact. For example, some business sectors operate under federal mandates to provide employees with periodic training. One company requires yearly training on ergonomic computer practices, and one municipality requires every heavy industry type of business in the city limits to conduct yearly fire extinguisher operation classes. However, in a disaster, with everyone wading through flood waters on their way to higher ground, the various authorities would probably overlook these sorts of mandates. So there is no need to put these at the top of your disaster recovery plans. And, your employees will be grateful that they don't have to review the primary causes of carpel tunnel syndrome yet again.

Others, such as payroll, are necessary for continued operation. Unless you are a self-funded start-up routinely running short of cash and delaying paychecks, employees need to be paid, even if your business is operating in contingency mode. Surprisingly (and sadly) few people have the means to easily weather even a short gap in pay. Your employees might understand if an event on Thursday delays Friday's pay. But they will become much less understanding if a week goes by without a paycheck.

Other business functions are mission critical. Even a brief absence of any of these systems could have a severe impact on your operations. Companies engaged in e-commerce may find themselves losing millions of dollars in revenue for every hour of downtime. These types of business functions need to be the focus of your recovery efforts.

A team of representatives from each area of a business—the people who work with these systems on a daily basis—should be the ones making the assessments of application and data criticality. First they must identify the criteria that define criticality. Then they must apply these criteria to the applications and data. After their assessment, they need to circle back and present their findings to management for review, bickering, and approval.

SCRAPPY BCP FAILURE STORY: *So how critical is a project timeline, really? Consider this anecdote, pulled from an article that appeared in Continuity Insights magazine. "This construction firm acted as the prime contractor on numerous buildings.... The construction firm did not own its own headquarters, but shared space with a dental office and a bank. Unfortunately for them, the dental office had a malfunction in its laser equipment, causing catastrophic smoke and water damage to the data center. This also wiped out the company's e-mail server. All of the company's critical documents—from engagement letters to bid proposals to submitted bids—were housed on these servers.... There were backup tapes stored offsite, but this information couldn't be recovered fast enough to stay on schedule.... The staff really tried to pull together, striving to bridge the huge gap in knowledge between company and personal e-mails. Some honest contractors were helpful, and shared information about their end of the project. Others exploited the situation and readjusted their take on the project, gouging the company on their services. But without any* *record of the transactions, and with everyone scrambling to keep their heads above water, it was tough to root out these problems. The company could probably have survived these issues if it weren't for the loss of project schedules. These project timelines had to be reconstructed from bits of paper and aligned with subcontractor schedules. This caused a series of mistimed construction problems."*[8] *As I will mention later in the section "Strategic Analysis," if it's that important, back it up real-time, offsite.*

3. Determine System/Application/Data Recovery Order

Naturally, mission-critical applications and data must be restored first. For a hospital, that may be patient records systems. For a bank, that may be online banking systems. Before you try to determine the system of highest priority, though, consider dependencies and timing.

Dependencies: Critical applications may rely on input from an application with a lower priority. For instance, an online banking application is a primary customer interface. As such, management might consider it the number-one recovery priority. However, it requires input from the customer information file. If so, restoring online banking will not get you back in business unless the customer file is recovered first. Critical interdependencies often are overlooked, which can be a costly mistake. ATM users won't be happy to find the ATM machine working, but saying, "Who are you?" because it is unable to recognize their bank card and access their account.

Timing: Criticality can depend on the relative timing of the crisis to the business operation calendar. Therefore, time-dependent operations should be ranked by temporal criticality. Your business may have a reconciliation job that absolutely has to be run...at month's end. So if the outage happens on the third day of the month, you have a reasonably long window for restoring this application. On the other hand, an application that is only run once a year might, upon initial investigation, be rated as low priority, but when it is needed, it is *essential*. As such, if the interruption were to occur during that application's "prime time," recovering it must be a top priority.

---

8. Ted Collins, "Surviving Business Disruptions." Downloaded 8/30/2010 from
   http://www.continuityinsights.com/articles/surviving-business-disruptions

While your initial consideration might be that recovery time objective (RTO) should be based on the immediate financial impact, potential losses can ultimately depend on the timing and extent of the incident. A better measurement of recovery priority may be the capability of each business unit's ability to continue to service customers using alternate procedures.

An "application recovery priority survey" is a useful tool that can be used to establish recovery order. Below is an outline of what should be in such a form.

The first section of the survey should list the application and owner information:

- Application ID/name (use a drop-down list to avoid inconsistencies)
- Application owner's name
- Application owner's department
- Physical location of application
- Platform on which the application is loaded

NOTE: For external applications, all vendor information—names, contact information, and the technologies they have supplied—should be catalogued to assist replacement of hardware and software.

The application owner, working in concert with people familiar with the use of the application, next should answer questions such as:

Business Function

- What functional areas does this application support? Example: *Sales* or *Manufacturing*
- What business functions does this application support? Example: *Manage facilities* or *Process payments*

Business Impact

- What type of adverse impact would there be if this application were unavailable? Example: *Negative publicity* or *Loss of customers*
- What type of adverse financial impact would there be if this application were unavailable? Example: *Fine* or *Loss of revenue*
  - Does the financial impact depend on how long the application is unavailable?
  - If so, what is the impact per day, hour or minute?
- What would be the maximum financial impact if this application were unavailable?

Temporal Impact

- What is the maximum length of time your department could tolerate lack of this application? (This is where the pain threshold, defined earlier, comes in handy.)
- What would be the work backlog duration from a five-day interruption?

Interdependencies with Others

- Who would notice if this application were unavailable: internal or external parties?
  - Who would be impacted by the unavailability? This determination may be different from those who would notice. For example a credit card customer may not notice that his card doesn't work for several hours if he doesn't try to use it during that timeframe.
- Does this application depend on input from another department, external party (*e.g.*, a business partner), or technology?
  - What is the application's data source?
  - How frequently is the data used by this application normally provided?
  - How is the data obtained: paper, email, remote access download, tape, disk, etc.?
  - Which person in the department receives or retrieves this data?

- Does another department, third party (*e.g.*, a business partner), or technology depend on the output from this application?
  - Who or what receives or retrieves this application's data?
  - How frequently is the required data generated by this application?
  - How is the data transmitted: paper, email, remote access download, tape, disk, etc.?
  - Who is responsible for the application that receives or retrieves this data? (This person or group may be different from the person or group who receives or retrieves the data.)

Current Contingency Plans

- Have you developed or established any alternative procedures?
  - Are they in writing?
  - Have you tested these procedures?
- Is the data backed up?
  - How often is the data backed up?
  - Where is it stored?
  - Have you tested the restore process? (If not, are you *stupid*?)
  - Have you tested the accuracy and completeness of any backed-up data? (Same snide comment as before.)

If this sounds like a lengthy, agonizing and tedious process, rest assured that it needn't be. Be creative! Get a budget for doing this over margaritas, or a membership at a local golf course. No one will mind filling this out on the break after the 9th hole.

Section 2: Operational/Financial Impact

What would be the type of operational and/or financial impact if this application were interrupted for five (5) business days? Remember some impacts will increase exponentially as time passes. Please consider the worst-case financial or non-quantifiable impact.

Please take into consideration not only the impact to your area, but also the impact to other areas dependent on this application. First, indicate the type of impact an interruption would have. Next, the amount of the monetary impact. Then, consider the non-quantifiable impact type and the related ramification, using the classifications of major, intermediate or minor.

3a. Quantified: What type of adverse financial impact would there be?

☐ No Impact
☐ Fine/Penalty Impact
☐ Cost Increase Impact
☐ Revenue Impact
☐ Stock Value Impact
☐ All Impacts

3b. Quantified: What would be the estimated financial impact for all impact types identified above? Please designate only one financial impact amount for the worst case impact or an estimated total for multiple impact items.

○ less than $250K
○ $251K – $999K
○ $1M – $10M
○ $11M – $30M
○ $31M – $75M
○ $76M – $100M
○ more than $100M

4a. Qualified: What would be the non-quantifiable impact?

☐ No Impact
☐ Communication Impact
☐ Privacy Impact
☐ Security Impact
☐ Regulatory Impact
☐ Employee Impact
☐ Reputation Impact
☐ Customer Impact
☐ All Impact

Done   My Computer

Graphic 1: Application Recovery Priority Survey Example, Part 1

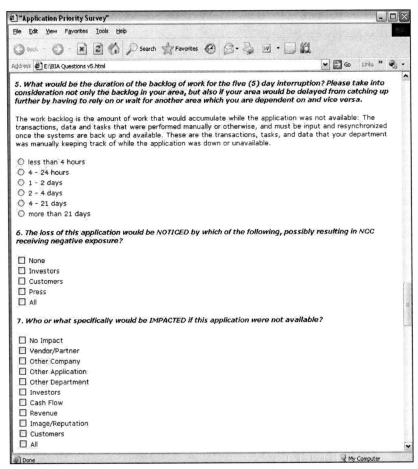

5. What would be the duration of the backlog of work for the five (5) day interruption? *Please take into consideration not only the backlog in your area, but also if your area would be delayed from catching up further by having to rely on or wait for another area which you are dependent on and vice versa.*

The work backlog is the amount of work that would accumulate while the application was not available: The transactions, data and tasks that were performed manually or otherwise, and must be input and resynchronized once the systems are back up and available. These are the transactions, tasks, and data that your department was manually keeping track of while the application was down or unavailable.

- less than 4 hours
- 4 - 24 hours
- 1 - 2 days
- 2 - 4 days
- 4 - 21 days
- more than 21 days

6. The loss of this application would be NOTICED by which of the following, possibly resulting in NCC receiving negative exposure?

- None
- Investors
- Customers
- Press
- All

7. Who or what specifically would be IMPACTED if this application were not available?

- No Impact
- Vendor/Partner
- Other Company
- Other Application
- Other Department
- Investors
- Cash Flow
- Revenue
- Image/Reputation
- Customers
- All

Graphic 2: Application Recovery Priority Survey Example, Part 2

After collecting the application recovery data (and posting the ranking of golfers who participated), weigh each response in order to prioritize the applications. Ultimately the final decision for this ranking rests with senior management, as the questions are more strategic in nature. What is the organization's greatest concern?

- Loss of customers?
- Negative media attention?

- Financial loss?
- Regulatory sanctions?

The first answer is usually that "everything is important," but that's nonsense, and the Scrappy BCPer doesn't settle for this response. (Kindly see chapter 7 of *Scrappy Project Management* by the editor of this book for more guidance on how to deal with this inane response.) In order to properly triage in times of crisis, you need to know the relative priority of these business concerns. Ask "What if?" questions to force execs to imagine making the tough tradeoffs they may actually face during a crisis. For example, you might ask "If you had to choose between a financial loss of $1M USD and extremely negative media attention, which would you choose?" Through a process of such pair-wise comparisons you can help your executives discern the relative priority of a list of items where everything seems to be worthy of #1 status.

Once management's "pain points" are understood, assign a numeric value to each response—greater concerns earn a higher score. If you've accurately captured the concerns and priorities of your business, once the numbers are tallied, the recovery order should align with the strategic importance of the applications.

4. Determine the "Pain" Threshold

Balancing the cost of contingency planning, and the cost of recovery when an event occurs, requires an understanding of the risk senior management is willing to take, and the pain that they are willing to endure. Maximum allowable downtime (MAD), aptly named, and maximum tolerable downtime (MTD) are two approaches for examining external commitments, such as customer needs, service level agreements, and regulatory requirements.

For example, the loss of online banking would cause some customer dissatisfaction. On the other hand, consumers are not surprised by an occasional, *"We're sorry, our website is temporarily offline"* message. Besides, financial institution customers tend to be loyal, in part because of the difficulties associated with changing banks. As a result, some downtime might be tolerable, and not result in customer loss and the associated negative financial impact. Of course, if the media reports that a bank's website was unavailable for an extended period, that negative publicity could lead to losses as current and prospective customers take their business and dwindling funds elsewhere. In contrast, downtime in the medical arena is much less tolerable. Imagine a patient in an operating room, under anesthesia, awaiting the surgeon, ready for the knife, but with no records. An outage in an online patient record system is not only intolerable, it is unallowable. A surgeon needs a patient's history immediately.

5. Determine Existing Vulnerabilities

There is no need to wait for a disaster to start benefiting from your BCP program. Once your assets are identified, examine their vulnerabilities, the potential threats against them, and possible countermeasures to protect them. This exercise typically reveals some previously unrecognized weaknesses in the business. Common vulnerabilities include:

- Poor physical and logical security, which allows access by insiders or outsiders who may be careless or have malicious motives.

- Insufficient maintenance, which can encompass both the physical environment, such as excessive dust, as well as a failure to maintain backups.

- Inadequate user and administrator training, such as failure to stress strong passwords, clean desk policies, and the threat of social engineering, which is an outsider's efforts at weaseling information out of your employees in order to gain information he then can use to compromise your systems.

The universe of existing vulnerabilities that you could discover through your analysis is limitless. If your operations center lies in a flood plain, you are susceptible to natural disasters like the previously mentioned "thousand-year flood" that struck Nashville in 2010. Or you may come to the realization that mission-critical applications are run on an obsolete hardware platform for which replacement parts can only be found in remote regions of the Sudan. Or perhaps your organization doesn't do a very good job of promptly patching systems, exposing the organization to both malicious attack and potential recoverability challenges. Yadda, yadda, yadda. You get the idea. Then, fix the no-brainers.

6. Establish Configuration Management

One way to mitigate a specific type of system vulnerability is to establish a configuration management process. Configuration management often is confused with change management. The latter is a business process that ensures changes to a system are reviewed for negative impacts before the change occurs. Configuration management, in contrast, is the process of cataloging or recording the history of all changes to hardware and software, both at the enterprise *and* desktop levels. Software, right out of the box, usually is configured for ease of use rather than security, and generally not configured to meet your organization's specific business needs. Over time the software ages like a distinctive cheese, and updates and patches are released and applied. Unnecessary services of the application usually are disabled at the server operating system level. In short, the application you have now is nothing close to what you had three years ago. Failure to document such changes will hamper, if not doom, your recovery efforts.

7. Examine Potential Threats

One of the most challenging tasks of BCP development is identifying and cataloging the threats against your organization. Answering the question, "What events could have a potentially negative impact on our operations?" is not simple. Threats to your systems can include a person (a system cracker or a spy), a thing (a faulty piece of equipment), or an event (a fire, flood or terrorist attack) that exploits a vulnerability of a system.[9]

Although negative thinking is rampant in the corporate world, people sometimes have difficulty imagining the dark side. Groups tend to find it easier to be more negative, feeding off of each other's dark sides. So gather a bunch of the most pessimistic, negative thinkers that you can find into a room and hold a "Doom and Gloom" brainstorming session.

9. Russell, D. and Gangemi Sr., G.T. 1991. *Computer Security Basics*. Cambridge: O'Reilly.

To make it interesting, offer prizes for the biggest threat, most politically incorrect threat, most threats, most unusual threat, most surprising threat, most socially unacceptable threat, and so on. Run an online contest in your organization to get everyone thinking negatively. People really seem to enjoy thinking negatively, so capitalize on that! If you don't believe me, just try sharing a truly breakthrough idea at your next group meeting, and see how long it takes before you are swimming in a sea of reasons why it will never work. Ouch! That's gonna leave a mark!

Once potential threats are identified, the next step is to rate the likelihood of each event. Humans are patently inept at estimating the likelihood of rare events (as evidenced by how many people fear flying but drive at the drop of a hat). Actuarial tables can offer some guidance here. These tables list the expected frequency of events such as earthquakes, power outages, locust plagues, and disk crashes. Though I mention it here and in the subtitle, the fact is, drives *will* crash. Count on it, and make sure your IT department has processes in place to mitigate the effects.

But even an event that has a one-in-a-million chance of happening may be worth preparing for if the consequences are intolerable. After all, it doesn't matter how low the risk of getting cancer from smoking is if you're the one who gets it.

Regardless of how you get your numbers, you will need to rely on something more scientific than "gut feel." The simple truth is that people are notoriously bad at understanding probability theory, as mentioned previously. To illustrate, consider that every statistics 101 book contains a variation of the following problem:

Let's say you flip a coin nine times, and nine times in a row it comes up heads. Which is more likely on the next flip...heads or tails?

A large percentage of people will say "Tails." When asked why, their response will be something to the effect of "It's due." Others might say "Heads," because "It's on a roll." The answer, of course, is that neither heads nor tails is *more* likely to come up, as the previous nine flips have no bearing on the tenth. It still is a 50-50 proposition. Heads and tails are equally likely in the next flip.

In addition, people also confuse possibility with probability. The latter is a percentage. The former is binary: something either is or is not possible. Read and reflect on the following passage, pulled from *An Introduction to Factor Analysis of Information Risk* (FAIR), a white paper on a risk assessment methodology:

Consider the difference between playing Russian roulette with a standard six-cylinder revolver versus a semi-automatic. The possibilities are equal with either handgun—i.e., it's 100% possible in both cases that the player would suffer a "negative outcome." The probabilities, however, are significantly different. In the first case, assuming the revolver is loaded with a single bullet, the probability of a negative outcome is about 17%. In the second case, assuming a single bullet is loaded and chambered in the semi-automatic, the probability of a negative outcome is about 100% (it might, of course, misfire). Clearly, I'd rather not play the game at all, but if I had to choose between the two weapons, I'd much rather base my choice on an understanding of the probabilities, as opposed to just the possibilities.[10]

Or, to be less gruesome, consider that the weather person does not (or should not) say there is a 0% possibility of rain tomorrow. Of course it is possible, even in Yuma, Arizona. It just has a very low probability.

The bottom line is that you should not worry whether it is *possible* that an airplane will fall on your facility or a major server will crash. It *is* possible. Anything is possible. And as our editor, Kimberly Wiefling, frequently spouts, "Everything *seems* impossible until your competitor does it. Then it's *merely* difficult." Don't worry about whether something's possible. Instead, worry about how *probable* the event is.

After establishing the probability of negative events, you will need to rate their potential impact and then create appropriate countermeasures. Proper countermeasures can minimize the effects of even a catastrophic event. For example, a data center may be in a tornado-prone area. However, if the center is housed in a hardened bunker below ground—and you have real-time backup to a site in an

---

10. Jones, J. "An Introduction to Factor Analysis of Information Risk (FAIR): A framework for understanding, analyzing, and measuring information risk." 2005. Downloaded 6/18/2008 from
http://riskmanagementinsight.com/media/docs/FAIR_introduction.pdf

area that would not be affected by the same storm—then the potential impact from data-loss perspective is negligible. Facility and human loss, of course, are a different issue. But dealing with the risk to human life is well beyond the scope of this book.

Below is a sample risk assessment form that you could use to capture and rate potential events:

Risk Condition	Descriptions Consequence	Probability	Speed of Onset	Predictable	Forewarn	Depts. Affected	Mitigation Effort	Action Taken
		1 = Low	1 = Very slow	1 = Always	1=Y		1 = low	Research
		2 = Medium	2 = Slow	2 = Sometimes	2=N		2 = medium	Accept
		3 = High	3 = Fast	3 = Seldom			3 = high	Manage
				4 = Not				Avoid
								Lower
								Eliminate

Graphic 3: Risk Assessment Form

Think outside of the box. When considering threats, it pays to look around. Your facility may be secure, but certain neighbors may be obvious threats. It's not hard to envision how a chemical plant or an armory could suffer a catastrophic incident which could affect adjoining locations. A little peripheral vision will serve you well.

In fact, secondary impacts or "collateral damage" are often the hardest to assess. Planning for "the unknown" represents a greater challenge. As the currently vogue phrase attests, "You don't know what you don't know." At first glance, a conference center might seem to be a safe neighbor. But, if it hosts a controversial event, protesters might spill over and prevent your employees and suppliers from reaching your facility. Something as innocuous as a house of worship could be the target of a hate attack. A Midwest manufacturer may not consider hurricanes a threat, unless it relies on ocean-going vessel shipments that must pass through storm regions. Oh, and who ever thought to put "volcanoes" on their risk assessment prior to the huge disruption in air travel from the big volcano in Iceland?!

8. Evaluate Countermeasures

Countermeasures are methods of protecting people, facilities, systems, and information against specific threats. Periodic data backups are a countermeasure against the threat of data loss. A sprinkler system is a countermeasure against a facility fire, and a gas discharge system protects against data center fires without destroying electronic equipment. Providing your employees with laptop PCs—and requiring them to take them home at night—is a countermeasure against equipment loss, and (if they are backed up to a corporate server somewhere) personally maintained data loss.

When reviewing critical assets, consider built-in safeguards. Then take the analysis one step further to see if additional protections can be added with minimal effort and cost. Obviously the countermeasure should not cost more than the potential loss, and they must not unnecessarily impede the conduct of business. That's the job of the information security guys. (Just kidding again!) As has been lamented many times, in many places, the most secure computer is never turned on, not plugged into anything, and buried in concrete one mile underground.

9. Review Audits

Another source of input for your risk assessment (primarily your technology risk assessment) is the results of recent audits, whether performed by internal staff or external resources. Internal auditors should evaluate your systems against defined standards, such as ISO 27002 (formerly ISO 17799). These ISO standards are guidelines for implementing and maintaining information security management programs. You might think a sophisticated audit would reveal sophisticated problems. But an audit using established standards and best practices frequently reveals mundane threats such as systems that do not use sufficiently strong passwords (increasing your risk of attack from an external entity), systems that are not patched regularly (also increasing your attack risk, as well as configuration management issues), or systems that are not backed up often enough. Do you really want to explain to your boss and executives after a devastating loss that the cause was weak passwords? When we do fail as BCPers, let's fail for new and more exciting reasons!

10. Focus on the Loss, Not the Event

The point I would like to stress in concluding this section is that business contingency plans should formulate a response to the *result of* an event, rather than to the event itself. Actions should not be based on a type of disaster—such as earthquake, terror attack, or flood—but rather the *consequences* of the disaster, and how the business should respond to those consequences. If your employees lose access to their workspace, it doesn't matter whether it is due to flood, fire, or pestilence. Your plan doesn't need to figure out how to deal with pestilence. Your plan needs to find another place for those employees to do their jobs.

Focusing on the loss greatly simplifies the challenge of BCP. A fire could destroy as little as a room or as much as an entire facility. A contained fire might have a negligible impact on operations. Therefore, it makes no sense to have a plan for a generic "fire." In contrast, a catastrophic fire, a chemical spill from a train traversing adjacent tracks, or a massive snowstorm on a Sunday night are entirely different events. And yet, the result is the same: Your employees cannot access your facility the next day. Therefore, plans should deal with events such as those which deny employees access to the facility, no matter what the cause.

In addition, plans should provide incremental responses for various kinds of business interruptions, ranging from minor inconveniences to worst-case scenarios. Anything less than a complete disaster can be dealt with using a subset of the worst-case plan.

The bottom line is that your plans should be geared towards what can be lost: a facility, power, suppliers, data, time, and—unfortunately—people.

SCRAPPY $0.02: *Do you really need a "volcano plan?" A recent report by a well-known research group (which I won't name, as I don't want to publicly embarrass them) said that you should have one, just in case a volcano in Iceland erupts again. Admittedly, a lot of commerce across Europe was impacted by the travel restrictions/cancellations resulting from the April 2010 of Eyjafjallajökull. So, great, you write a "volcano plan." But what if the next massive travel disruption is caused by gale-force winds whipping across Europe for a week? Or a labor strike by the folks who deliver jet fuel? Or a plague of locusts darkening the skies between CDG and FRA?*

The above speaks exactly to the point which I already have made, but will repeat: plan for the result, not the event.

Strategic Analysis

"However beautiful the strategy, you should occasionally look at the results."
- Winston Churchill

Once you have identified vulnerabilities and prioritized potential risks to your business, it's time to get busy creating your plans for responding to them. Your plans will begin to take shape as you consider enterprise-wide concerns using the approach recommended below. Key areas include:

1. Research and Establish Backup Storage Alternatives
2. Research and Establish Recovery Alternatives
3. Establish Lines of Succession
4. Establish Disaster Criteria
5. Consider Small Disasters
6. Establish Disaster Declaration Criteria
7. Establish Relationships with Local Emergency Services
8. Develop Communications Plans
9. Establish Plan Distribution Strategy
10. Establish Return-to-Normal Criteria

1. Research and Establish Backup Storage Alternatives

We've all heard the cry, "Don't put all of your eggs in one basket." Those of us who keep copies of important documents in a bank safety deposit box practice this strategy in our personal lives. For a corporation, the reasoning is identical. Aside from the intentional threats faced by high-profile organizations, all businesses face data loss due to accidental events such as hardware failure or natural disaster. If a threat, or a range of threats, exists for data in one location, then putting a copy of that data in another location is a sensible strategy for minimizing the potential for loss.

Several years ago, data backup was a lot more challenging than it is today. Lower-cost data storage, additional storage technologies—such as CDs, DVDs, USB hard drives, and thumb drives—and increased data transmission speeds provide more options for data redundancy. But, even with advances in backup technology, it's still not a simple endeavor.

SCRAPPY NEAR-DISASTER #1: *The need for a data backup strategy applies at the PC level as well as the enterprise level. A certain scrappy editor friend of mine almost lost a book she was writing when the laptop on which it was stored—the only place it was stored—experienced "issues." Fortunately, some "percussive maintenance" saved the day. She got the computer working again by dropping it from about one meter high. While it's understandable when "commoners" get caught with their pants down like this, it simply wouldn't do for a BCP professional to be unprepared for such an event. In contrast, while writing this book, I kept copies of my progress on my desktop PC and a thumb drive that I took to work. To add "suspenders" to my "belt" protection, I frequently copied a version to my ISP's online file storage system.*

As already mentioned, the backup technologies you should employ depend on your pain threshold. Daily archiving (a high-level buzzword is near-continuous data protection or near-CDP, which is a fancy term for a point-in-time snapshot at a set interval) might be fine for some businesses, but if your organization simply cannot afford to lose any data at all, then a nightly backup is insufficient: real-time database mirroring (continuous data protection or CDP, not surprisingly) may be the best choice.

Regular testing of backups is an often-overlooked step in the process. If your backup media are corrupted or incomplete, then there is no backup, and your contingency plans are just illusions, with no more substance than a politician's promise.

SCRAPPY NEAR-DISASTER #2: *I recently attended a conference where the keynote speaker related this anecdote. Back in the days of 5 ¼" floppies, a system engineer was dismayed to learn that his entire series of backup disks was unreadable. In troubleshooting the system, he duplicated his process, checking each step along the way. After creating a set of backup disks, he asked a secretary* *to label and store the duplicate set. He watched in amazement as she affixed a label to a disk, cranked the floppy disk into the carriage of her typewriter, and typed on the disks! Do not assume that each step in a backup process will work until it has been thoroughly tested.*

A Few Words about "The Cloud..."

Depending on whom you ask, cloud computing is either the best thing to come along since 1s were invented to go along with the 0s in our computers, or the worst thing since NBA players discovered Twitter. For a business contingency planner, it's probably somewhere in the middle.

For the benefit of the three or so people on the planet who have not yet heard the term, cloud computing is using the Internet—"the cloud," as that is how it often is depicted in network diagrams—as part of your computer system. Computing, in this case, ranges from:

- Using a third-party application that is not hosted at your corporation, but rather somewhere else. WebMail is a good generic example. GoogleDocs is a specific example. This arrangement is referred to as "software as a service," or SaaS.

- Putting one of your own applications out there somewhere so it can be accessed over the Internet. This use is called "platform as a service," or PaaS. An imperfect analogy would be an online banking system. The reason I call it "imperfect" is that online banking is *supposed* to be accessed by people via the Internet, whereas platform as a service is really about your employees accessing an internal application which is hosted somewhere other than your data center, facilitating its development, delivery, maintenance, and use.

- "Borrowing" computing resources, such as processing power and storage from a third party. "Infrastructure as a service" (IaaS) is a great tool for organizations which have certain peak periods when their computing needs spike—such as an online retailer during the holidays—to handle the additional workload without committing resources which would then sit idle, or under-utilized, the other 11 months of the year.

- If you want to go all-out, consider desktop as a service. DaaS involves putting everything—applications and user data—on the servers of a third-party service. The user's work-in-progress is copied to a "virtual desktop" at login, and back to the cloud at logout. The beauty of this arrangement is that access to the company's data does not rely on a specific PC, network, or even location. And you don't need to worry about updating each computer's applications as they're all synced to the central applications. Sounds like an IT person's dream come true!

If your mission-critical data is stored on a third party's servers, then you've definitely gotten it offsite and out of harm's way, should a local disaster take place. (Or have you? More on that later.) But it's still not a panacea.

First, if the local disaster is a power outage at your facility, and if there's insufficient backup power to run your networking equipment, then you still can't get to your data.

Second, consider bandwidth needs. A dedicated line between your primary and backup sites will be able to move more data, more quickly, than even a fast Internet connection. And if the amount of data you have and use can be measured in the tons, then to restore it all might require something as quaint as tapes.

Third, you have to carefully vet the service provider. Will they be around in five years, when that disaster strikes and you need to get your data? How good is their security? Who are they? (For all you know, WeBackYouUpAllYourStuff.com is owned by some eastern European criminal gang, which will troll your files for sensitive information.) *Where* are they? A cloud computing operation could have servers all over the country. So what happens if they decide to store your data on a server in a building that just happens to be across the street from your facility? You've just lost your "Godzilla distance."[11]

---

11. A colleague and I once had a discussion about backup facilities. His thought was that it had to be sufficiently far away so that Godzilla couldn't stomp on both during a single rampage.

Fourth, bear in mind a point raised throughout this book: backed up data does not equate to a business contingency plan. If your data is there, but all of the computers needed to access it have been destroyed, or the people who know what to do with that data are not available, then you have...well...nicely backed-up data.

Finally, many organizations are bound by HIPAA or GLBA compliance requirements. Putting your data into the hands of a third party simply may not be an acceptable option.

As an excessively paranoid information security (infosec) professional, my opinion is that cloud computing can be a great cost-saving measure. And I'm sure it's the wave of the future. But if, for not too much more money, you can store your data offsite and keep it under your own control, the decision should be obvious.

Let me conclude by pointing out that there really is no such thing as "the cloud." There are different kinds of clouds and different ways to use cloud computing. The National Institute of Standards and Technology (NIST) offers a whitepaper which defines and demystifies cloud computing.[12] Among the "flavors" described is the "private cloud," which is controlled by the organization. That's nothing more than an offsite, Internet-accessible storage facility.

2. Research and Establish Recovery Alternatives

Unless your business is completely virtual, with no physical facility whatsoever except your employees' homes (hopefully more than one), a business contingency program should incorporate the use of an alternate facility. While working from home may be an option for some people, if there is an event which prevents normal operations at one of your facilities, then having another work site—at a sufficient distance so as to not be affected by the same event—gives employees who need a facility a place to work.

There are several types of alternate sites. Two of the most common designations are "hot" sites and "cold" sites. No, this has nothing to do with the climate where the site is located or the temperature control of the buildings. Although these terms are fluid, generally speaking, hot

---

12. http://csrc.nist.gov/groups/SNS/cloud-computing/cloud-def-v15.doc

sites are emergency facilities that effectively duplicate an organization's operations: facilities, computers, and data. In theory, your employees could walk into such a facility, sit down, and immediately resume normal operations like standing around the water cooler. Aside from their favorite coffee mug or pictures of loved ones on desks, this is more or less like a parallel universe where everything has been duplicated, including the dysfunctional politics.

In contrast, cold sites offer computer-ready space with desks and cabling, but no computers. Think of this as a partially furnished apartment. You may have a couch to sit on, but there's no TV to watch and nothing in the refrigerator. For some of you this may resemble your home environment more than you care to admit. Ten thousand channels of crap on the TV to choose from and some mustard in the fridge.

In between are so-called warm sites, admittedly not the most imaginative of names, which are equipped with computers, communications services, power, and environmental controls, but none of your precious data. Or, you could investigate using a mobile recovery center, which brings the computers and communications equipment to the designated location, kind of like the "Magic Bus" of the 21st century.

If the alternate facility that you choose is not in your home city, there are additional planning considerations. Although not required, your organization may want to make arrangements for employee food and lodging rather than having everyone make their own plans. Also, some employees may be accompanied by their families, especially in the case of a serious or widespread regional disaster (unless you're in Japan, where employees routinely live separated from family for their work). In contrast, if the disaster affects only your facility, employees may prefer not to disrupt family routines. (However employees with a newborn may think, "Yes! Time away from the screaming thing.") But, in the case of both employee and family relocation, a business usually can secure a better rate by reserving a block of rooms. Congratulations, you are now also in the travel agent business. The thrills never stop for us BCP peeps!

In addition to food and lodging, providing employees and their families with information about local amenities—such as gyms, day care, movie theaters, and other recreational establishments—will improve morale. Obviously, most people won't care about such niceties if they were fleeing for their lives. But in the case of less serious business disruptions, the gesture will be greatly appreciated. You'll be glad that you researched these services in advance so that you are not trying to track them down in the middle of a crisis, not that you would take the time to do this after the fact. But try to imagine dozens of children locked up in hotel rooms with their parents. Productivity will sink and all of your BCP relocation plans could be for naught. Do yourself a favor and consult the local chamber of commerce or "Google Maps" for guidance, putting together a plan before it's needed.

One fairly obscure detail to keep in mind is that many commercial hot sites have agreements with multiple clients. Their reasoning is that disastrous events—such as fires—affect only a single location. But, the most unimaginable things can and do happen. A regional disaster could result in multiple entities contending for the same resource. Other hot site providers specify only that they will provide a facility which meets the contractual requirements...but not *which* facility. As such, you could find yourself assigned to a site far from your original location, operated by personnel who are unfamiliar with your technical setup and business needs. Before contracting with an alternate facility provider, find out if it has multiple clients, and what their contractual obligations would be in the event of a disaster affecting multiple clients with conflicting needs. At the very least, make sure your business gets first dibs.

There are other options besides alternate facilities, such as maintaining multiple business locations in different geographical locations. Unused space at one facility could be designated for contingency use for another facility. At first glance, leaving a percentage of your business space unoccupied may not *seem* to be cost-effective. But it may prove to be less expensive than contracting for an alternate facility. Another option worth exploring is renting or leasing commercial space in an unoccupied office building. Many office property firms own multiple buildings that are wired, furnished, and temporarily vacant. You may be able to enter into an agreement for vacant space on an as-needed basis, wherever it happens to be available. However, the amount of vacant commercial real estate can

Chapter 3: Developing Your Business Contingency Program

vary, and options may be limited during an upward swing of the business cycle. (I've *heard* that those sometimes happen.) Yet another alternative would be entering into a cooperative agreement with a similar, but non-competing, business for sharing facilities in the event of a disaster. Be creative! After all, in the ideal world you'll never make use of these plans!

Whether using a commercial hot site or another solution, always keep security in mind. Just as criminals scan the obituaries to find the names of relatives of the deceased to determine when homes will be vacant for funeral attendance, it is not hard to imagine corporate criminals looking for similar opportunities to prey on businesses during a crisis. And scam artists, such as phishers, definitely look to take advantage of a business—or its clientele—during uncertain times. (Blatant commercial: if you want to know more about phishing and other techniques that scammers use, I would humbly suggest picking up a copy of *Scrappy Information Security: The Easy Way To Keep The CyberWolves At Bay.*)[13] Employees' awareness of security may grow lax amidst the chaos of a real business disaster, so consider the following:

- IDENTITY - If you are sharing a facility, how do we distinguish "us" from "them." This distinction might not be easy, since there could be temporary help brought in to replace those who could not relocate. Hand out unique badges—ideally, ones that feature a photograph—to identify employees, temporary employees, and consultants to keep the rabble out.

- ACCESS - Your logical access controls may present challenges as well. You may have some employees performing other people's jobs. If Zack is suddenly doing Sheena's job, but he does not have access to the same computer resources as Sheena, then he cannot do her job effectively. Temporary employees will need access to the computer systems, too. Some challenges may be alleviated if your organization uses role-based access controls (RBAC), since dropping user IDs into roles is easier than adding access on an *ad hoc* basis. Check it out and implement it. In this day and age of frequent job loss it's probably a good idea anyhow.

---

13. http://amzn.to/9P1DVj
   (www.amazon.com/SCRAPPY-INFORMATION-SECURITY-PLAIN-ENGLISH
   -ARCHITECTURE/dp/1600051324/ref=sr_1_1?ie=UTF8&s=books&qid=
   1244223145&sr=1-1)

- INFORMATION - Clearly, sensitive information needs to be kept secure. The need for security includes PCs, removable memory, and documents as well as other sensitive materials, such as discarded documents, damaged hard drives, or memory media—which are headed for the recycling bin.

- PROTECTION - Assuming that your primary facility was not a total loss, you will need to provide security there as well to prevent theft, vandalism, and corporate espionage. (Yes, people would actually stoop to this.)

3. Establish Lines of Succession

Ask yourself "What if the entire management team of your organization were on the ill-fated flight American Airlines flight that crashed into a Queens neighborhood in 2001?" Although it is human nature to avoid considering such an unpleasant possibility, it is conceivable that the person—or persons—in charge of your organization could be incapacitated or killed in a disaster, or even in the normal course of daily life. A recent example would be the April 2010 crash which killed Polish President Lech Kaczynski and more than 80 of his country's military and political leaders; music aficionados might point to the February 1959 crash which killed Buddy Holly, Ritchie Valens, and "The Big Bopper." Consider that the President and Vice President of the United States are never allowed to travel in the same vehicle. Chances are your company has no such rule for the CEO and the top people. Therefore, it is critical to establish a line of succession so that a decision-making structure is sustainable after such grim events. (After all, you don't want to see your company's version of Alexander Haig claiming that *he's* in charge broadcast on the nightly news.) Remember that while senior executives are critical to long-term strategy, many essential day-to-day decisions are made by much lower-level people. In order to keep operations running in the long-term you'll need to develop alternative command lines for all mission-critical departments and functions.

4. Establish Disaster Criteria

Remember the H1N1 virus? It was an illness, then one day it became a plague. Some big shot just declared that it was, and all kinds of things changed as a result, including the time it took to get through customs in Japan (or so I'm told by my editor, who travels there frequently). So, when exactly does a difficulty become a disaster? In the event of a catastrophe—such as the destruction of a facility or a widespread natural disaster which devastates an area—it's pretty clear, and to some extent, decisions are easier. In such cases, moving operations to a backup facility is a foregone conclusion. But, if the event is less than catastrophic, decision-making becomes more challenging.

What if a meteor only falls on *half* of your facility? If a facility suffers extensive, though localized, damage from a quickly contained fire or other disaster, can operations continue (safely, of course) in the rest of the building? In some cases, yes, and in some cases, no. Were dangerous fumes or other materials released by the blaze and subsequent fire-fighting? Can displaced workers be relocated within the facility, or must they move to another building entirely? Activating the backup site for a small contingent of employees could be expensive and appear unnecessary in retrospect. The cost of the contingency plan will linger long after the urgency of the crisis fades from memory. Further, a backup facility has workstations, but not *their* workstations with *their* work-in-progress. So relocating also would entail moving their personal hardware, which may be difficult to justify after the smoke has quite literally cleared. You may have your judgment called into question after the fact—or worse—find yourself punished for your good deeds. Oh, darn.

Another minor disaster would be a power outage. Of course many facilities have backup generators sufficient to provide power to critical areas such as mainframes and servers. But there might not be enough current to power everything, such as lights, air conditioning, and individual PCs. At the very least, if mainframes and servers can continue operating, and your employees are using laptops, they should have an opportunity to save crucial data or even, perhaps, continue to work for a limited amount of time after power is interrupted. Make sure they are trained to spend time doing that in addition to texting friends and family their status.

5. Consider Small Disasters

What if you are located in the middle of a Cleveland winter and, while the electricity is flowing and things are otherwise humming along, the heating system goes out? That could chill employee enthusiasm, pardon the pun. In many areas offices generate so much heat that cooling is more of an issue than heating, so maybe you could get by with some simple huddling of the masses. But, what if the HVAC goes out? Humans might be able to tolerate the sweat running down their backs, but heat-sensitive computers may experience operating problems. And, unless employees are used to working in a tropical rain forest, some might find the work environment unbearable after several hours. Also, it only takes a couple of hours without water—for drinking or more importantly, for flushing—to render your facility unpalatable, if not unusable.

To underscore that point, take a look at a real email I received from our corporate communications group at 10:30 one morning.

Due to a water main break in downtown Cleveland, there is not sufficient water pressure to operate our buildings downtown. Other facilities in the area are being assessed and their status will be shared as more information is known.

As a result, the downtown facilities will be closed at 11 a.m. this morning. This evacuation is mandatory. Employees in essential business functions will be expected to relocate to alternative locations according to their contingency plans. Other employees are expected to work from home if possible.

At this time, we expect these buildings will be closed for the remainder of the day. And, we expect the buildings to reopen tomorrow morning as usual.

Later in the day came the following update.

Water pressure has returned to normal at all but one facility in downtown Cleveland.

Though there is a boil alert (*Allegedly witty intermission: I'm not sure exactly what that is, but I don't think it was an irritating skin condition.*) extending through 6 p.m. Thursday, facilities in downtown Cleveland are expected to be operating under normal working hours on Thursday, though employees should expect to rely on bottled water for drinking, rather than drinking fountains, until the boil alert is lifted.

As a reminder, employees should stay in touch with their managers for the latest information about individual work locations and schedules.

Another example of a small disaster is a telecommunications outage. These days most organizations conduct a significant amount of internal communications via email or instant messaging. While the loss of internal communications can be frustrating, there are alternatives, some of which could even improve work performance. One that I've heard of is called getting up from your desk, walking over to the guy across the hallway, and having a face-to-face conversation! Come to think of it, maybe you should induce a telecommunications outage now and then just to promote improved relations and break the addiction most people have to email. Or, just be direct and establish—as other organizations have done—"email-free Fridays." (I'm already feeling the withdrawal symptoms just *thinking* about it!) Internal communication is critical, of course. However, depending on your business, the loss of external communication could be termed a serious disaster with dire consequences. Imagine a taxi service in the suburbs unable to receive phone calls. Imagine an online software provider unable to accept orders over the Internet. Imagine iTunes down for a day. Cha-ching!

Even though it may seem a bit melodramatic, I will use the term "disaster" to refer to any disruptive event for the rest of this book. Clearly, though, your exact response depends on the extent of the event, which could range anywhere from mishap, misfortune or reversal, to a calamity or a downright catastrophe.

6. Establish Disaster Declaration Criteria

Figuring out when to officially declare an event a disaster is not a simple matter, the movie *Ishtar* notwithstanding. The complete and utter destruction of a facility is an easy call. If the building is gone, it's pretty black and white. Employees *will* report to the alternate site. But, what if there is a chemical spill at 6:00 p.m., and clean-up is estimated at 12 to 24 hours? Now you're into more shades of gray than a conservative businessman's closet. Twelve hours is just inconvenient; 24 hours means you either relocate or lose a work day. Bear in mind, relocating for even a single day entails significant costs. By what time do you need to let employees in on your plans? (We'll discuss how to communicate with them a little later on.) Further, if you do decide to pull the trigger with your alternate site vendor, most commercial alternate sites have a set fee for power-up, even if you change your mind and your employees never show up.

Ultimately, the decision to declare a disaster and begin operating in contingency mode belongs to senior management. If you are not one of the top dogs, make sure you have a way to contact them, or you may find yourself operating way out on a limb during the decision-making phase, and hearing a disturbing sawing sound shortly thereafter.

7. Establish Relationships with Local Emergency Services

Ideally presenting yourself as the "chief contingency officer" (CCO), make sure that you introduce yourself to government officials in your home city well ahead of any nasty situations, emergencies, or other unsavory events. Schedule appointments with the mayor, chief of police, fire chief, and city services director. Familiarize yourself with local regulations and disaster plans. Establishing a trusting relationship with local agencies before disaster strikes will pay off big when you need their help, or heaven forbid, have to walk in hat-in-hand and answer for some disaster caused by your company.

Getting to know the mayor is helpful because he or she is an overall point of contact for interaction between your organization and the city. Becoming acquainted with the police and fire chiefs will make it easier for them to contact you in an emergency as well. A nearby chemical disaster could quite literally spill over and affect your operations. For example, a hostage crisis at a neighboring business could prompt police to close adjacent streets, impacting your operations. The city service director can make you aware of any utility work conducted in your area. On occasion, construction results in ruptured water, gas, or power lines. Armed with prior knowledge of work in your area, you can send a message out to your work force alerting them "Today, especially, save your work often." Come to think of it, even without nearby construction, this might be a useful message to send when the backup practices slacken! Just keep a jackhammer in your office and set it off a couple of times during the day to support the ruse.

8. Develop Communications Plans

A BCP program is useless without a way to alert people when it's executed. A business contingency plan must include an employee notification tree. If you're relying on telephones, don't put your pencil down quite yet. While making telephone calls may seem straightforward, telephone service may be overwhelmed in a disaster—as often is the case during an evening rush-hour snowstorm, or on Mother's Day—or physically disrupted—as was the case on 9/11. For events that affect only your facility, clogged communication lines would not be an issue. But, a regional event could bring down the communications network entirely. Consider providing key personnel with satellite phones. Yet another method of contact could be through the Internet. A record of employees' home email addresses could provide a means of alternative contact. If email is part of the notification plan, make certain your employees know to check their email. Or you might consider a private Facebook page, Twitter, or something Twitter-like, such as Yammer. Remember, you are in the business of planning for the worst, and the human link is often the weakest link.

SCRAPPY TIP: Use social media! Over 500 million of the world's 900 million computer users now have a Facebook account. Technically speaking, it's the third-largest nation on Earth. While not world class or secure by any means, even small businesses could set up a social media group, such as a Yahoo! Group or other such service to enable quick and easy IM notifications in the event of a problem with company email.

Don't forget to include suppliers, partners, and customers in your emergency communications plans. A tractor-trailer full of parts arriving at an empty plant is not only embarrassing, but costly. A thorough stakeholder analysis of everyone who'd care about a disaster, everyone who could help you, and everyone who could hurt you, might reveal some important players you've overlooked.

SCRAPPY BCP FAILURE STORY: *I found this tale on the website of an IT, security, and BCP solutions provider: "A Galveston-based bank initiated steps to prepare its business in the event a cata-strophic hurricane came through the Gulf Coast. The bank created* *a continuity plan focused on addressing information security and employee safety. During Hurricane Rita in 2006, the bank executed its continuity plan only to realize one fatal flaw. After ensuring the safety of its employees and preparing its facility, the last step was to ship the backup hard drive to a protected location. What the bank didn't realize was that the post office, DHL, UPS and FedEx had already shut down business and evacuated the coast. Had the bank fully tested its procedures, it would have realized the crucial nature of that step.*" [14]

9. Establish Business Contingency Plan Distribution Strategy

Once your plans are developed and tested, devise a distribution strategy in the event they are needed. It should be obvious that storing your plans *only* electronically would hamper efforts to put them into action, but sometimes such obvious things don't become apparent until it's too late. Paper copies are a must. (Or you can go the Jason Bourne route, and plant the plans in a battery-powered subcutaneous device, but count me out if you expect me to surgically remove it myself when it becomes necessary.) The lack of a hardcopies of your BCP is the kind of easily overlooked detail that comes to light only during a thorough exercise of your plan.

Even if every employee has a laptop with emergency plans stored on them, your company is not necessarily covered in case of a disaster. Certainly, in almost every disaster scenario, one electronic copy of the plan stored on an individual laptop outside of the affected building would suffice. But, what about an event like the Great Northeast Blackout of 2003? While laptops can run on battery power for a while, your plans could, and should, be dozens of pages long. Without power to run printers, your employees' only recourse would be to copy it to paper manually. Quickly. VERY quickly.

---

14. Downloaded 8/30/2010 from http://bit.ly/bSNsdS
    (www.rsacorp.com/index.php/business_technology_solutions/business_continuity_planning/)

Hardcopy plans must not only be printed, but distributed. Again, that task may sound simple, but it poses two challenges:

- CURRENCY - Developing business contingency plans is not a fix-it-and-forget-it exercise. Plans must be updated regularly in response to organizational change and changes in the external environment. Although your "January plan" may have substantial overlap with your "June plan," there may have been significant changes. At the very least, the notification tree will be obsolete.

- SECURITY - Business contingency plans offer a candid look at the details of your organization's business processes and infrastructure needs, specifically your weaknesses and vulnerabilities. What would happen if your plan fell into the hands of your competitors? What might a rival pay for such a document? Ensure that your plans are protected. In fact, uncontrolled access to business contingency plans is one of the most significant challenges facing BCPers.

Please don't go running into the night screaming "There is no hope!" But there are no magic solutions to contingency plan currency or security problems. Trusted key individuals need to have access to these plans, and, in fact, play an integral part in creating them. How do you ensure that your plans are up-to-date, secure, and yet available when needed?

The currency issue is easy, but time consuming: someone in your organization—either in the contingency planning office or at the departmental level—must be charged with updating and periodically printing and distributing copies of the plan. (Gee, now that has to rank right up there with refilling the pocket protector stock in the office supplies cabinet.) Plans also should be delivered to, or printed at, your alternate facility sites on a regular basis.

Security is harder. But then again, security *always* is harder. Awareness is the key. Make sure that your employees understand, in no uncertain terms, that the business contingency plans that they possess are highly confidential corporate documents, as sensitive as any strategic plan or intellectual property. Business contingency plans must be securely stored and disposed of just like any other sensitive document. Of course a distribution list must be maintained, and employees should be required to turn in their old plans when new ones are issued, or when they leave the company, so that you can verify their destruction.

10. Establish Return-to-Normal Criteria

The final strategic decision in a disaster is determining when it is over. This signals the return to normal operation. In some cases, it's a trivial decision. For example, a snowstorm might hit on a Thursday night, shutting down operations on Friday. In most cases, by Monday operations should be back to normal. Or, after an electrical outage, once power has been restored and the facility and its systems are judged to be in working order, the business can begin the journey back to normal operations.

However, as is almost always the case, even apparently straightforward situations can contain surprising complexity. Suppose your organization's primary facility was destroyed and then rebuilt. Employees could return to work and resume normal operations in the new digs. However, any facility move entails some disruption, and usually a fair bit of extra work for the employees. If the availability of new facilities happens to coincide with a business-critical time period—such as end-of-quarter processing—then it might be prudent to complete the critical tasks at the alternate site, rather than adding the chaos of a re-relocation. In any event, someone declared the official "disaster," and someone needs to call it off. Make sure it's clear who has the authority to send the "all clear" signal, and what the steps are to return to normal operation.

Plan Content and Subject Matter

"Failing to plan is planning to fail."
- *Alan Lakein*

Creating a business contingency plan is not rocket science. Actually, it is more analogous to a recipe. The challenge is knowing what ingredients to put in the pot. (Just ask Colonel Sanders or Captain Coca Cola.) But a recipe alone doesn't make cookies. Good contingency planners excel because they ask the proper questions. Anyone can fill in a checklist: "You need a PC-check. You need access to the shared drive copy of spreadsheet payroll.xls - check...."

To create an effective contingency plan, you will have to interview managers and employees to determine what they *really* do and what they *really* need. In this phase, you will:

1. Catalog Personnel Information
2. Catalog Job Functions
3. Catalog Business Processes: Daily, Weekly, Monthly, Etc.
4. Draft Detailed Standard Operating Procedures
5. Catalog Equipment Requirements
6. Develop Manual Procedures
7. Establish Call Trees
8. Cross-Train Job Functions

1. Catalog Personnel Information

Beyond our job functions, each of us has personal skills, deficiencies, tics, and quirks that may not be relevant on a day-to-day basis, but in contingency mode, might be significant. The questions to ask are literally limitless. Search for both vulnerabilities and strengths, as illustrated in these examples:

- Do you have someone—either a child or a parent—who relies solely on you?
- Do you have a medical condition—diabetes, heart condition, disability—which requires regular attention? In asking that question, though, be careful to not run afoul of privacy laws.
- Do you know CPR?
- Do you own a car? Those who rely on public transportation may need special arrangements.
- Is your car large enough for carpooling?
- Do you keep your tires sufficiently inflated? (OK, perhaps that one has no real-world bearing.)

Naturally you'll need to steer clear of invading privacy and legal faux pas when inquiring into employees' personal lives. Seek guidance from your legal department on this. And, to minimize misunderstandings, make sure the people you interview understand that the purpose of your questions is to help protect them in the event of an extreme situation.

Guide your employees through a mental rehearsal of various crisis scenarios. Ask them to consider a situation, and then visualize the next step. This exercise, as with many in contingency planning, is not a one-time event. Encourage your employees to pay attention to their daily routines for any details that may prove to be valuable—or risky—in a crisis.

SCRAPPY TIP: A business contingency planner must learn the right questions to ask when cataloging personnel information: does a team member drive a large four-wheel drive vehicle, and live near other employees? Information like that could be of assistance in the event of a snow disaster. Once, while asking an employee to list any personal information that she thought could be relevant, she said, "I faint at the sight of blood." We laughed, but that would be good to know and share with those likely to be around her so they would not wonder why she passed out. And we sure won't ask her to help out on the medical response team!

Of course, practice through testing will reveal more details. Testing will be addressed more thoroughly in other parts of this book. For now, consider that conducting a disaster simulation exercise should help uncover these types of details.

2. Catalog Job Functions

Most employees have a job description that was prepared by a manager, modified by human resources, and presented to us at our interview. Whether in written form or not, we agreed to it by accepting the job. And it was accurate until about our second day at work. But just as projects often experience scope creep, workers experience job creep.

For example, Harvey was hired to catalog widgets. Someone left and Harvey assumed his or her duties on the widget review committee. Someone saw an example of Harvey's writing and asked him to handle communications for the widget committee.

Over time, Harvey streamlined and refined the cataloging process, developed a database to track widgets, and learned the identity of the internal communications department person to help with widget announcements.

These details and functions exist only in Harvey's head, and perhaps also on his laptop, rather than as a shared resource. If something were to happen to either, these processes could be hampered or lost.

Therefore, it is up to you to work with Harvey to tease out what he really does beyond his standard job description. This will be an on-going process, since Harvey probably will not be able to recall them off the top of his head or laptop, but will remember the details as he does them.

As with other organizational processes and applications, there is a strong possibility that Harvey has some task that he performs regularly, but infrequently. Typically, a lot of things happen at the end of the month and quarter. (A lot happens at the end of the year, too, but it's usually burning the use-it-or-lose-it vacation days.) Business contingency planners should encourage employees to keep the BCP task in the back of their minds, so that when they perform one of these infrequent functions, they note it.

SCRAPPY TIP: Regrettably, there is no complete and definitive list of Scrappy BCP questions that you should ask. Experience—and a healthy dose of paranoia—are your best drivers.

Although this book has an entire chapter devoted to the "Power of Negative Thinking," you needn't spend all of your time on the "Dark Side." Let's focus for a minute on the positive. One method you can use to tease out these kinds of details is the appreciative inquiry process, developed by David Cooperrider and Suresh Srivastva in 1986.[15] At a high level, appreciative inquiry involves talking about what works well about a process to determine why it works well, and then applying those lessons to other processes.

3. Catalog Business Processes: Daily, Weekly, Monthly, Etc.

Asking individual employees to list and explain their jobs will uncover most of your organization's business processes.

To continue the example above, Harvey is involved in various aspects of widgets. But who runs the nightly widget inventory reconciliation? It could be an automated process. But if so, then some department owns it. And, most likely, the owner only thinks about it when there is a breakdown or other unusual event: out of sight, out of mind.

In a large company there may be dozens, and perhaps even hundreds, of these types of widget processes: nightly batch jobs, month-end reconciliation, and end-of-year adjustments. They might have been scripted, thereby becoming "invisible" processes, remaining ghostly shadows until some server upgrade results in the assignment of a new IP address, which causes the whole thing to grind to a frightening halt …usually at 2 a.m.!

---

15. http://appreciativeinquiry.case.edu/

SCRAPPY TIP: When things do come crashing down, make sure someone notes what caused the crash, and what was done to "un-crash" it. Those details will be important during a disaster.

Just as with job functions and personnel details, it is your job to ask the kinds of questions that uncover these invisible processes and catalog them. Just ask something simple like "What do you do on the last and first days of the month?" And also ask, "Experience any surprises lately?" These kinds of questions give your colleagues a chance to pause and reflect on the value and impact of their work, something most harried employees have precious little time to do. Some of them may even thank you for it.

4. Draft Detailed Standard Operating Procedures

There is some overlap between this step and the previous two. The distinction is that after listing individual job tasks and enterprise-wide functions, your subject matter experts must then perform a "deep dive" to determine the specific details of each. If you really want to be well prepared for a disaster, you truly should have the SME go into agonizing, and even gory, detail. The final product should be analogous to assembly instructions for a bicycle or a bookcase. For example:

1. At 9:00 a.m. every day, the widgets manager retrieves SPREAD-SHEET.XLS from the shared server (path name = //shared-drive/accounting/widgets/).

2. The widgets manager visually reviews SPREADSHEET.XLS for an out-of-balance state, which occurs when there is an un-matched credit or debit. Matching credits and debits always will appear within five rows of each other on the spreadsheet.

   a. If there are unmatched transactions, the widgets manager contacts the counting manager in the Counting Department. The counting manager should check previous day's order sheets (stored by increasing timestamp order on the shared server (pathname = //shared-drive/orders/current-year/current-month) to confirm the discrepancy. The counting manager will correct the error in SPREADSHEET.XLS and post a new spreadsheet, notifying the widgets manager when complete.

3. The widgets manager takes the error-free SPREADSHEET.XLS and runs the macro "Reconcile," which appends data from the database SALES MASTER (path name = //shared-drive/sales/), saves SPREADSHEET.XLS and sends email notification to the widgets adjuster in the Adjustments Department.

4. Etc.

At the lightning speed that many businesses change, you can imagine how frequently this kind of detailed information becomes obsolete, Yup, pretty much immediately. That's another reason that BCP is a field only for the tenacious and the obsessed. Only a Department of Defense treatise on the proper disposal of weapons-grade plutonium could exceed the anal retentiveness of this process. And, chances are, if you're lucky and you live right, you'll never make use of this excruciatingly detailed process. But you might find a boatload of inefficiency hidden in standard processes that could be eliminated even in the absence of a disaster. Look for that kind of ROI (return on investment), and use these examples to build more support for your BCP initiative.

FROM THE SCRAPPY HEADLINES: *When interviewing employees about the specific of their jobs, they might slip up and reveal something similar to these two tawdry tales.*

"Over a period of nine months, the number of computer malfunctions within a large company had risen from an average of two per year to critical levels.... Secret surveillance equipment was installed to monitor staff. One was filmed lightly scratching circuit boards in disk units and also attaching paper clips to them. Both these actions led to a short circuit. When confronted, he confessed everything. His motive was to earn overtime, which was required to process the overlap work which was delayed by the malfunction."

"A series of incidents occurred during one night shift at a major computer installation. A series of power-downs prevented further output as there was no engineer present to re-initialize the system. Shift staff consequently had to be sent home each time. The cause

was eventually discovered. An operator was so jealous of his unfaithful girlfriend (allegedly!) that he discovered a way of 'checking up on her.' On random occasions he would turn the mains switch off and then back on again, and would subsequently be sent home...unexpectedly. The idea occurred to him following a genuine failure." [16]

Though you probably wouldn't add those to your plans, reporting them might earn you some points on Mahogany Row.

5. Catalog Equipment Requirements

Just as an army "marches on its stomach," the modern office runs on its equipment. Atop nearly every disk sits a PC. Near the little blinking light that tells you it's alive is the cable that connects it to the servers and mainframes that hold the data that we use on a daily basis. Replacing this "big iron" and the data they contain should be part of your overall data backup plan. Your backup strategy may be shoving files to offsite storage by some physical means. Or, it may be data mirroring. With mirroring, in the event of a disaster, at the flip of a switch the backup servers become the primaries. Either way, your data should be safe and sound. It is safe, that is, *if* it has been tested, as stressed in the "Application Recovery Priority Survey" in the section "Determine System/Application/Data Recovery Order," and bludgeoned again in the section "Research and Establish Backup Storage Alternatives." Just make sure you test it. Don't get caught with your pants down on this one!

Replacing PCs, while not trivial, is relatively easy. If your employees use laptops, you should establish a policy that requires them to go home each night (the PCs, not the employees...well, both, actually). Or, require that a specific percentage of each department's employees take theirs home, not that this will be easy to monitor or enforce. With most or all of your laptops offsite, if a disaster strikes after hours, the need to replace PCs is reduced, if not eliminated. And, you will save the mission-critical data that—despite your policies, protestations, threats, and bribes—*is* stored at the PC level.

---

16. Downloaded 8/27/2010 from
http://www.disaster-recovery-guide.com/stories.htm

Though some employees might lament having to schlep their laptops home every night, remind them of the simple math that the odds favor a disaster occurring outside of the 8–5 weekday window. If reminding fails, threaten to take away their laptops. (OK, better save that one for after you quit in disgust. There hasn't been anyone tarred and feathered for a while, but it could happen.) Or try this carrot: if tomorrow winds up being a "snow day," you can work from home, rather than burn a vacation day. Of course, make sure your policies and training explicitly state that, one, laptops should be transported in the trunk of their cars (or locked in the passenger space if they don't have a trunk due to driving an SUV, hatchback, or sports car with a trunk the size of a pocket watch), and, two, they should be brought *into the house* at night. I once led an incident response team meeting to review the case of a laptop stolen from the employee's car, which was parked in the driveway over night. Gee, would you leave $1,000 in cash lying in your car overnight in plain sight? Not likely. Were it my decision, that employee would have had his laptop privileges revoked. Or at least he would have been required to leave his wallet lying on the seat beside the laptop each night.

Keep in mind that the recovery site strategy you choose might eliminate the need to replace PCs: a hot site, as described previously, may have desktop units ready in the event of a disaster at the primary work site.

SCRAPPY TIP: If your recovery strategy relies on using retired, or mothballed PCs, ensure they are updated and patched. If some departments require specialized software, have it loaded on the backup PCs in advance or scripted so it can be installed as quickly and painlessly as possible. Otherwise, your employees may find themselves trying to work on the logical equivalent of a Commodore 64. (If you don't know what that is, you're young and have a wonderful full life ahead of you. Congratulations.)

By now, you might be thinking, "Servers...check. PCs...check. We're in business, right?"

Wrong!

Although mainframes, servers, and PCs are business drivers, do not forget peripherals such as printers, scanners, faxes, and other equipment. The paperless office is still a pipe dream. Granted, when operating in disaster mode, your employees can be told to forego convenience documents like meeting agendas, attendee lists, and recipes pulled from the Internet. However, there will still be a need to print the documents required for business operations. For example, a real estate office must have the ability to print and fax signed documents to continue working.

Your job as a planner extends beyond the computer. Remember to ask, "In addition to your PC and data, what equipment do you require to perform your job?"

6. Develop Manual Procedures

Even in today's modernized, homogenized, and computerized enterprise, a surprising (OK, I'll stop) number of critical functions can be completed without the benefit of PCs, intranets, and databases. The trick is diving down into the business process to see what is really being *done*, and then developing alternatives.

Consider the call center of a financial institution. Clearly many customer inquiries cannot be answered when systems are down. A balance inquiry is a prime example. But consider some of the other reasons a customer might call. He might want to change an address, or request that a new addition to the family be added as a beneficiary. And some credit card companies allow customers to choose their own billing cycle end date, so they might call to update that.

In all cases—disaster or not—a customer service representative's job is to verify the caller's identity and right to alter personal information, and then record the details, make system entries, and save any changes. How can these procedures be implemented in the absence of a working system? With pen and paper. As repugnant as this possibility might be, would you rather alienate 100% of your customers or only a portion of them? It's your call, but a BCPer is in the business of removing excuses, not providing them.

Consider the change-of-address request as an example. Online, the primary display provides multiple prompts for identification: customer first and last name, current address, monthly payment amount, and account numbers, for instance. (To someone like me, who works for a financial institution, it's obvious. But, suffice to say, you *really* need to make sure that you're talking to the right person before you change the address of record for a customer.) When the customer service representative verifies the customer's identity the representative moves to the change-of-address entry display. When that information is entered and submitted, the transaction is complete.

So how could a call center do all of that without functioning systems? As part of developing their contingency plan, the call center manager should dump all data entry screens into separate documents, save them as e-documents, and print copies. Both electronic and paper versions should be distributed to the staff. Of course that means that the customer identification process documents also have to be available in some kind of hardcopy format unless, of course, your people know all of your customers personally.

If a caller were to ask for an account balance while a business is in contingency mode, the representative would have to tell the customer that the systems are down. However, if the customer simply wanted to submit a change of address, the representative would have options. If just the network were down—but PCs were still functioning—the representative could retrieve the electronic version of the form, ask the usual verification questions, and then *log* the new information for later data entry. Once the systems return to normal, the identity information is compared to make sure it agrees, and if so, the change is made. If the IT department is really sharp, the representative should be able to automatically update the database directly from the document, rather than manually transfer it field by field to the system.

If the call center is experiencing a problem where *all* systems are unavailable, the basic process is the same as above, though the CSR would have to utilize the paper form and, regrettably, manually enter the changes later.

Obviously it's a heck of a lot easier not to be down, right? So just make sure your back up systems work and you won't have to face this paperwork nightmare.

However, if you do implement such a paper process, be sure to include instructions for the proper disposal of paper documents after they are no longer needed. Otherwise, your next disaster will be cleaning up the public relations nightmare stemming from somebody tossing a ream of paper with customer names and account information into a dumpster. (Everything can and does happen.)

To be sure, alternative processing methods present challenges from both security and privacy standpoints. But remember, the enterprise is facing a *crisis*. The wolves are at the gate, the iceberg is looming. So if the alternative is *not* doing business, then operating at "half speed" is preferable to closing the doors. The risks can be mitigated somewhat if your organization has established and regularly follows best-practice procedures for functions like address changes, such as sending a confirmation letter to both the old and new addresses.

7. Establish Call Trees

If a disaster impacts your business during working hours, your employees—at least those who are onsite that day—will probably know about it. (One would hope!) In a best-case scenario, everyone will evacuate, meet at the appointed locations, and be tallied. Although it is usually the task of managers to contact absent employees, the office grapevine, sped by cell-phones and text messages, will also circulate news of the disaster to employees who are not there at the time. In fact, the latter probably will beat the official word to those who are not there.

As mentioned previously, if the facility is not totally destroyed, the all-clear notice can take from minutes to days. What would be the waiting period until employees are dismissed to go home (or wherever)? When should they come back? If the disaster takes place during off-hours, what is the employee notification procedure? Who knows? And how will they know?

The answer is a call tree. A call tree is a cascading list of who calls whom to get the word out to all stakeholders. The simplest way to implement a call tree is to follow the organization chart. The department director calls his direct reports. Each of them calls their employees down the chain. The last person calls somebody near the top to confirm that they message was received. In some companies this will be the first time a regular employee gets to call one of the top dogs. It could be the highlight of his or her career. Don't undersell this important perk! You might even want to fire off some practice call trees to improve skip-level communication if your organization has a problem with communication up and down the hierarchy.

Having multiple phone numbers for each employee increases your chances of reaching them. Also, make sure that all employees—especially the managers, or those "high up" on the list—have easy access to all of the contact information for at least one other chain to ensure that there will not be a scramble to get the phone numbers of Luke's "callees" into Suki's hands, should efforts to contact Luke fail.

Like any other component of a contingency plan, you should test your the call tree on a regular basis. Make it fun! There's no reason this needs to be some tedious task. Use it to announce the profit sharing percentage for the year, or the date of the holiday party, or the winner of the BCP "Dark Side" Negativity Contest. Be creative!

SCRAPPY TIP: It sounds obvious, but make sure your employees actually understand the call tree process. I have heard several anecdotes about call tree tests which broke down. In one case, the test was publicized in advance. Everyone knew about it. But one department's test failed. Why? Because the second person in the tree got the call, and went back to watching TV, reasoning that the announced two-hour time frame for the exercise left him plenty of time to make his calls after the movie was over. He failed to realize that those further down his chain had to call others—and so on and so forth—all within the two-hour period. In the other case, the employee received the call on his cell phone, only to realize that his list was in the car...about a 30 minute walk away since he and his family were spending the day at an amusement park. Never underestimate the power of misguided assumptions to scuttle even the best-laid plans.

Phone numbers—even cell numbers nowadays—are relatively stable. Nonetheless, send out an updated contact list periodically—once per quarter, for example—and specifically *ask* for updates. A single break high enough in the call tree structure can mean that dozens or hundreds of employees are not notified. Of course you'd be a fool to trust updates to this voluntary process. Some low-paid college intern may be able to proactively verify the phone numbers of everyone on in your list in just a couple of days.

8. Cross-Train Job Functions

In a large organization, certain tasks must be done by multiple employees; a 50,000-employee business would be hard pressed to have only one person who handles user account maintenance. (Unless he has 12 arms and never sleeps.)

In a disaster, some of your employees may not be available to fulfill their duties. In a severe disaster they could be injured or dead. Aside from mortal consequences, there may be other reasons for absences. Some may be unwilling or unable to work at the backup site because of its distant location. Others may be members of the National Guard and required to help with a disaster response. Or they may put family welfare above that of the business and say, "to heck with it." Whatever the reason, they may not be there. Deal with it!

To minimize the impact of absences to your business operations, you should establish a program of job cross-training. While limited resources may prevent your organization from having a backup employee for every job, make sure critical functions are understood and can be completed by more than one person. After all, no pro football team has only one quarterback, and many have an emergency QB—someone who plays another position, but takes a few snaps in practice every wee—in case the first-stringer and his backup both go down with injuries in the same game.

Cross-training programs have other benefits. Disasters aside, people leave abruptly. If multiple employees can perform a given task, that knowledge does not walk out of the door with the departing employee. Also, teaching employees new skills can increase job satisfaction and employee engagement, something proven to increase your revenues and profits, by preparing them for possible advancement within the corporation. Cross training doesn't have to be an onerous exercise. Simply designate a backup or two for each critical position, put them in a room with the subject matter expert, and let him or her review the detailed standard operating procedure documents with the backups.

Having the backups shadow their key person can add even more value to both your organization and your employees as they develop a greater understanding of, and appreciation for, the work that their colleagues are doing.

Let us chant together yet again, "This is not a one-shot exercise." Schedule such sessions regularly to keep the backups current and fresh.

Emergency Response and Operations

"If you can keep your head when all about you
Are losing theirs and blaming it on you...
Yours is the Earth and everything that's in it,
And—which is more—you'll be a Man, my son!"
- *Rudyard Kipling (and not Marie Antoinette)*

Depending on the scale of the disaster, the response may involve the assistance of entities outside of your organization. To enable emergency responders to be effective, you should develop a separate plan (that is, separate from your BC plan) to:

1. Identify the Command and Control Requirements of Emergency Management
2. Identify Potential Types of Emergencies and the Required Responses
3. Develop Emergency Response Procedures
4. Provide Status Communications.
5. Ensure Emergency Response Procedures Align with Public Authority Requirements

If a disaster occurs, your first consideration *always* should be the safety of people—employees, visitors, suppliers and customers—and not just because they will sue you if they are injured, especially if you are located in the USA. It's just the right thing to do. A proper business contingency plan includes emergency procedures focused on the safety of people. Emergency response plans are generally developed at the enterprise level, in contrast with individual plan development, which takes place at the department level.

1. Identify the Command and Control Requirements of Emergency Management

Somebody must be in charge. That person—or persons—must evaluate the nature and significance of the emergency. The emergency response leader must decide when to call for an evacuation and when to call the various authorities. And, that person must decide the destination of evacuees, a topic that is further addressed in the section "Develop Emergency Response Procedures" later in this chapter. In most cases it is unlikely that the emergency response leader will be a member of senior management, as they will have bigger fish to fry. Most likely it will be the senior security officer on duty, or the building manager. In short, it will be someone onsite and able to assess the situation—ideally, someone *trained* to make such an assessment—who will make the call. Once external emergency responders arrive, they are the authorities in charge, and assume the position of emergency response leadership. (That could be your cue to evacuate, my friend!)

2. Identify Potential Types of Emergencies and the Required Responses

A point which bears repeating is that business contingency plans should detail the response to the *result* of a disaster, rather than the disaster itself. The same is true of emergency response plans. Evacuating a building is evacuating a building, whether the threat is a fire alarm, an actual fire, a chemical spill or a bomb threat. Consider potential events that would lead to an emergency at your facility, determine the likelihood of each, and develop logical plans which take into consideration the subtle differences in the results of each possibility and how the response must be adapted for those differences.

As an example, consider the devastating results of the 9/11 tragedy. When the first plane hit the north tower, the two immediate threats to occupants and people nearby were smoke and fire in the building, and debris falling to the street. Because of the danger caused by the shower of debris, occupants of the South Tower were told to stay in their offices. That would have been sound advice if there had not been a second plane. Clearly the emergency response leader didn't consider that another plane was targeting the second tower, and that both could collapse entirely. Sadly, hindsight is 20:20. In retrospect, immediate evacuation would have been the most prudent course of action for all survivors in both towers.

3. Develop Emergency Response Procedures

Every business facility in the United States should have an evacuation plan that is regularly tested with all employees, even those complaining, *"I'm on an important call! I can't take part in a fire drill now."* If your facility is located near a hazardous business—such as a chemical plant, refinery or other not-so-friendly places like munitions plants, rail lines, and airports—the evacuation plans should offer much more specific advice than "Run the other way!"

Evacuation plans usually will overlap with emergency response procedures. High-level considerations include:

- ESCAPE ROUTE AWARENESS - Are exits clearly marked? By law, they must be, but have your employees been trained to find the nearest one, as well as look for alternative exits? Remember how in an aircraft your nearest usable exit may be behind you? Same goes for a building, but in this case it may be above you, too.

- COMMUNICATIONS - Communicating in an emergency is a two-step process.

  1. How should employees notify the facility security team of an emergency?

  2. How should the security team notify the building's occupants?

Does your communications system have zone notification so that employees facing danger are evacuated, while others not immediately threatened are apprised of the situation, but told to prepare to evacuate? Many facilities, especially those outside of city centers, are sprawling complexes. For example, a hospital campus could be spread over many acres. At such a facility, a fire in one area might not justify evacuating the entire premises. In fact, a complete evacuation could be counterproductive, as people pouring from exits could be in greater danger, or hamper entry by emergency responders. (During a recent earthquake in Japan, one of the three casualties was a person hit by a truck while fleeing a building.) If your facility is larger than a typical house, you may want to include a provision for zone evacuation, which includes "invacuation" or "shelter-in-place," that is, preparing, but staying put until either given the signal to evacuate or hearing that all is clear. (Of course that won't help if there is a "second plane"....)

- SAFETY MARSHALS - In a small facility, the security staff may be able to stand in a central location and direct people to the nearest exit. In a slightly larger facility, they may need to make the announcement with a little more volume behind it. Remember to use your outdoor voice, or use electronic enhancement, preferably digitally altered to sound like somebody really important. In most cases, however, this is not a practical solution. Assign a team of trained volunteers to guide people to the proper exit, and then perform a work area and bathroom check to confirm that no one is left behind. Designate "sweepers" for each specific area to check for any remaining occupants, and then report in to the assembly area managers. At least that's how it's done at a certain Fortune 500 company with 2,000 people on their site. We interviewed one of the sweepers, who requested anonymity. Under duress he disclosed that his site also has an "ark" with enough food and water for employees to last for several days, as well as the most popular Wii Video games. I think he was just pulling our leg about the Wii video games.

- MEETING POINTS - An orderly evacuation can be compromised if evacuated employees get outside in the fresh air and then set off to seek out their friends, or worse, leave the premises to rescue their families, or just hang out at the beach. Assign each department a specific designated meeting point known to all employees. Use clear descriptions such as "the north driveway by

Main Street." You may even want to post signs clearly marking the meeting points for various groups. That's how the big guys do it. A designated meeting point serves two purposes:

1. It divides your employees into manageable groups, which speeds head count.

2. It directs people away from inappropriate cluster points, such as the main entrance, through which rescue workers may need access.

Actually, you should designate several meeting points at varying distances from your facilities. For example, in the event of a fire, your employees can assemble in the parking lot, far enough away to allow fire equipment access. In contrast, for a gas leak, employee meeting points should be located across the street or down the block. In the event of a hazardous materials spill, the meeting point might need to be much farther away. (Does anyone remember Bhopal?) The evacuation order needs to specify the nature of the emergency and the appropriate meeting point. Of course collecting people becomes a bit more challenging as the meeting point is farther away, especially if there is a pub between the facility and the meeting point.

- HEAD COUNTS - Many organizations use an "In/Out Board" to track employee whereabouts, but many employees treat tracking themselves casually. However, it's no exaggeration to say that, in a disaster, it could be a matter of life and death if rescue workers must search a building for someone who went to lunch without bothering to check out. So emphasize, emphasize, EMPHASIZE that signing in and out is as important as the day's first cup of coffee. In an evacuation, designate someone to tear the status board from the wall and bring it to the assigned meeting point to assist in an accurate head count. Better yet, get RFID sensors implanted into all personnel and let technology track them. (OK, it may be too soon for this little timesaver.)

- VISITOR AWARENESS - If your facility has a large number of non-employees—such as a mall or a hospital—an evacuation drill should include them, too. Many high-risk environments make visitors to the site review a list of emergency guidelines before entering, and one our editor visited even required each person to pass an exam on emergency procedures before granting access. Three strikes and you are out, by the way! If you don't pass the test you don't enter. Now THAT is scrappy BCP!

4. Provide Status Communications

In the minutes and hours after an event, you will need to communicate with both internal and external parties on a regular basis. At its simplest, this communication can be the "all clear" which tells your people that they may return to their offices. Or, if employees are sent home, they should leave knowing *what number* they should call, and *when* they should call, for updates. Good luck getting anyone back until at least the next day, however. Seriously, what would *you* do? Wait eagerly by the phone to be allowed back into your office?! If employees are sent home, they need to notify any external party who may have been planning to visit later in the day. And the postal service, couriers, and suppliers must be told to suspend or re-route deliveries until normal operations resume.

5. Ensure Emergency Response Procedures Align with Public Authority Requirements

While this concept was touched on earlier, below are some topics that you may want to discuss with local emergency responders:

* Does your facility present special or concerns, such as hazardous materials or an on-site day care center?
* Are there employees who require special assistance?
* Where are electrical, gas and other central controls?
* Are there places where evacuated employees should *not* congregate?

Time Is of the Essence

During an emergency, time is one of your most limited resources. Well-prepared emergency responders react more quickly, do things right the first time, and improve your chances of optimally dealing with the emergency. Prepare. Practice. Perform.

4 Plan Execution

I love it when a plan comes together."
- *John "Hannibal" Smith*

Executing a business contingency plan involves the following steps:

1. Situation Evaluation
2. Last Known Good Data Point Evaluation, i.e., Time of Last Backup
3. Make the Decision and Publicize the Announcement
4. Relocation
5. Clear Work Backlog
6. Process Resumption Using Alternative Facilities
7. Site Restoration
8. Records Maintenance
9. Completion of Site Restoration
10. Data Restoration
11. Relocation to Recovered Site
12. Clear Work Backlog (Again)
13. Resumption of Normal Operations

1. Situation Evaluation

The range of disasters and their impacts is limitless. A water main break, an earthquake, or natural gas explosion all happen without warning. Bombings generally are unexpected as well (except by the bomber), though in some cases there is some warning in the form of a bomb threat. Likewise, a power outage is an unannounced event. But when thunderstorms roll through an area, electrical outages can be expected, unless you live in San Francisco, where thunderstorms are so rare that people drop everything to stare out the window at the show. So if you hear the distant rumble, don't think, "Oh, I can wait a few more minutes before saving this document I've been working on all morning." (Or, if you live in San Francisco, "Oooh. Pretty lights. I'll just walk away from this document I've been working on all morning.") Should you save now? Yes, for pity's sake!

Finally, some disruptive events, such as snowstorms, floods, hurricanes, and labor strikes, usually "grace us" with several days' notice.

Not surprisingly, the first step in disaster response is to evaluate what happened, and then to determine what is *happening*. Let us examine a power outage as an example.

What happened? The power went out.

Why? There is a thunderstorm.

What should we do? Continue operations and wait it out. The power probably will be back on soon, and our very expensive emergency generators can keep the entire facility running at full power for six hours.

What if? If service has not been restored after four hours, re-evaluate the plan.

But if the power is out because an ice storm has brought down lines throughout the state, the response will be different. If electricity is not going to be restored for at least 24 hours, you cannot expect to run your facility at full power during the interruption. And if the outage is widespread, you cannot assume that your employees will have electricity at their homes either, which otherwise would let them access the operations center—running at a reduced capacity—remotely. If the outage is *extremely* widespread, even the alternate facility may not be operational. And if it's global, then it just doesn't matter, now, does it?

If the decision is made to wait it out, you'll want to get word to your employees right away. Being kept in the dark—both literally and figuratively—instills panic. Use the most appropriate communication method available, even if that means walking through the cube farm with a bullhorn. (Or hiring that guy who always sits behind me at the movies and telling him, "Just use your normal theater voice.")

Continuing the electrical outage scenario, you'd want to announce to your employees that the facility is operating on backup power so they don't sit there blow-drying their hair unnecessarily, etc. Ask them to shut down non-essential equipment, such as desk lamps, their coffee makers (hey, extreme situations call for extreme sacrifices), and peripherals. Explain that overhead lighting will be dimmed. Encourage/browbeat your employees to back up their work often during the power outage. If, after four hours, the power has not been restored, prepare them for the possibility of leaving and taking their laptops with them to more hospitable climes. If you have someplace that you post status messages in such situations, update it frequently so they can easily access the new information. And remember to contact your fuel supplier to see if they can make a special delivery to top off the generator's tanks, which would allow you to keep the power on a bit longer.

You probably get the point by now: set in motion responses to the disaster, re-evaluate the situation as it unfolds, and modify your responses based on the ever-changing nature of the emergency. And, remember, contingency plans are based on the results of events, not events themselves. Focus on the results, and likely further results, as the situation progresses.

SCRAPPY KUDOS: *For an excellent example of situation evaluation, look no further than "The Mouse." Whenever an earthquake strikes Disneyland, such as the 7.1 magnitude quake in April 2010, teams spring into place. The first step is getting guests off the rides, and treating any injuries. Then, all rides are closed and examined. The inspectors know what to look for, allowing them to complete their task, and re-open the rides, as quickly as possible.*[17]

2. Last Known Good Data Point Evaluation—Time of Last Backup

For the remainder of this chapter, the working assumption is that a disaster has rendered your facility unusable, leaving no gray area as to whether you need to evacuate. We'll assume that, at this point in time, you have not determined whether it is recoverable, will have to be abandoned, or rebuilt. That is the job of the site restoration/salvage team. Lucky them. Let's just assume that what *is* known is that tomorrow people will not be working there. A cynical person in a rather unproductive workplace might remark, "Oh sure, like they *ever* work there." But this is no time to joke. Just to cover all possible workplaces, let's say that your people won't be physically appearing at what was, until disaster rendered it unusable, a perfectly acceptable place to spend a weekday.

Get right on the task of determining the state of your mission-critical data. If your data is housed on distant servers, mirrored in real time, the answer is easy…well, maybe. Real-time mirroring would *seem* to offer the assurance that data cannot be lost. And, most of it will be preserved. But, if your employees' work-in-progress is performed on their desktop PCs—and those PCs were destroyed before mirroring was completed—then you do not have *all* of the data. On the other hand, if your systems force your employees to work from a shared resource, or if your employees were using laptops *and* they had time and the presence of mind to take them along, you may have all of your data.

---

17. "Earthquake at Disneyland" Downloaded 8/262010 from http://exm.nr/9ERsnB
(www.examiner.com/disney-in-national/earthquake-at-disneyland-what-happens-after-the-ground-shakes-at-the-happiest-place-on-earth)

At this point, your preparations, your equipment budget, your policies, and your employees' willingness to follow those policies all contribute to the success of your data recovery efforts.

3. Make the Decision and Publicize the Announcement

Once the designated authority within your organization has made the decision to begin alternate operations, the word needs to get out to your facility provider lickety-split. As mentioned, some alternate facilities rent to multiple organizations, and there is the possibility of contention for space. So the first step is to notify the recovery facility ASAP. The quicker your call, the better your chances of being the first ones in the door and back in business.

Once you have confirmed that the recovery facility is powering up, you will next need to notify your employees. If the disaster happened during business hours, they at least should know that something has occurred and will have to be dealt with. But they might have gone home before the relocation decision was made. (Indeed, many may not even know that an alternate facility *exists*. Another item to add to your communication checklist.) Or, if the event happened after hours—and did not make the evening news—your employees might be completely unaware of the situation.

The solution, not surprisingly, is to use the call tree you painstakingly compiled to tell your employees where to report. The business may be better served if certain employees work from home, while others work from the alternate facility, especially if having everyone at the backup site would mean stacking bodies to the ceiling. It may sound obvious, but make sure your employees know how to get to the facility. Tell them what they will need to bring, such as their laptops, personal effects, or other items to make working in a strange environment more comfortable. Inform them of the expected duration at the alternate site, especially if it sufficiently far away that daily commuting is not possible. They'll at least need to bring jammies, deodorant, and a toothbrush in this case. And let them know if there will be any unusual working hours—overtime, over night, or six-day work weeks—so they aren't taken by surprise once they are there. They will be harried enough. Why add to it by dropping a bomb like, "By the way, you will be working the midnight-to-noon shift...surprise!"

4. Relocation

The task of relocating sounds straightforward enough, and in many cases, it is: move from point A to point B. However, failure to consider the following could tilt the experience from just inconvenient to flat out miserable:

- Encourage your employees to conserve parking spaces at the alternate facility (as well as save the planet), especially if it is being shared with other businesses. It may even make sense to provide a shuttle service to the alternate site instead of having employees rely on their own transportation.

- If the facility is being used by other organizations, make sure someone is available to direct your employees to your work area.

- Managers should cluster their employees logically at the new facility, and make introductions between geographically dispersed employees who might have been working "together," and yet have never met.

- Check that there are enough desks to accommodate employees. If not, make arrangements for working in shifts. (A technique you could consider is "hot desking," which is an extension of the old Navy practice of "hot bunking," in which a sailor coming off shift takes the bunk of a colleague who is starting his shift.)

As soon as possible—perhaps even in advance, unless your back up facility is some big fat secret—provide your employees with maps showing the location of the alternate facility, as well as maps of the building interior to help them quickly acclimate.

5. Clear Work Backlog

Once the alternate facility is up and running, the first task will be for your employees to clear the backlog of work which accumulated between the onset of the disaster and the time that the alternate site became operational. If your business processes rely on prioritized tasks—for example, if order number sequence needs to stay in sync with a date/time stamp—your employees should clear the backlog *before* handling new work. If there is no such requirement, then the work *could* be performed in any order, though from a customer-service standpoint, you might want to process older assignments first.

6. Process Resumption Using Alternative Facilities

Once the backlog is cleared, begin tackling new work. Recognize that some team members may have to forego their normal duties to act as floating help, providing assistance where needed. Don't forget to provide sufficient low-tech office supplies in your contingency plans, such as paper, sticky notes (even in a disaster we can't work without those!), forms, staplers, paper clips, and the other office essentials necessary to keep a business running. And strong coffee and treats should be viewed as "office essentials" at your alternate facility.

7. Site Restoration

In parallel with establishing operations at an alternate site, your site restoration/salvage team should begin determining what must be done to restore operations at the primary site. In the event of a devastating situation—fire, building collapse, irreversible contamination—recovery may not be an option: you might be looking at a ground-up construction project or relocation. Of course, even if you don't have to move, there may be negatives associated with the original site—such as the inability to expand because of surrounding properties or its location in a hazardous area—that may make acquiring or building at a new site the preferred course of action.

For water-damage disasters, ranging from floods to water main breaks, recovery will entail clean up and restoration. Carpeting and furniture may be a total loss, but attention also should be paid to infrastructure, such as wiring and plumbing, which should be inspected and tested. IT equipment that was soaked may need to be replaced, along with software and data.

Even a non-disaster—such as a prolonged power outage in the middle of winter—may necessitate an evaluation to determine, for example, that no pipes have burst, which could lead to a "secondary" disaster once they thaw. It's bad enough when it happens at your home, but when the pipes are spewing water onto your server room after the disaster has been declared "over," it's enough to make a BCPer weep.

8. Records Maintenance

Let's face it, most of us have had the experience of walking from the TV room to the kitchen, and forgetting why we made the trip. So it stands to reason that, while working under stressful conditions, your people will lose track of the "small stuff." As such, you should impress upon your employees the need to maintain accurate records...by writing things down! Business records will be specific to individual departments, but three classes of record apply to all departments:

1. **Individual Work**. There may be a need to reconcile data, records, or orders once operations resume at your primary facility. Maintaining a record of who did what simplifies the task of correcting discrepancies.

2. **Personal Expenses.** Employees may have to pay for their own accommodations and food, and later file for reimbursement. Encourage them to keep a log of their expenses. Otherwise, they may forget a few-and lose the receipts-which only will complicate the task of paying them back. Of course it's cheaper if you refuse to pay them without receipts, but a reasonable per diem allowance can simplify the entire process on both sides.

3. **Lessons Learned.** Even if your company has been unfortunate enough to operate in contingency mode before, each situation is unique. Someone might find a "hole" in the plan. Someone else might discover a better way to divide the work. If no one records these types of lessons at the moment they were learned, such experiences may be lost, turning these precious gems into "Lessons Not Learned."

In all cases the point to remember is that, when operating under less-than-ideal conditions, the details will be forgotten.

9. Completion of Site Restoration

Once recovery crews declare the new facility operational—which should include completed inspections of electrical, plumbing, and HVAC system—it must be furnished, restocked, and communications and IT systems tested and brought online. Easy to say, but potentially a huge undertaking. Remember, money turns a problem into an expense. Make sure you have budget to get the job done quickly!

10. Data Restoration

Once the site restoration/salvage team has completed their work it is time to turn out the lights at the alternate digs and send your employees back to your primary site. If the disaster had no impact on your data center—that is, if you simply began accessing data from a different location—then the data restoration step is unnecessary. But if your recovery effort involved replacing data stores, prepare to migrate data from the backup servers to the restored primary servers. You'll want to ensure successful data migration using checksum processes. (Explaining checksums is beyond the scope of this book. That's what Wikipedia is for. And the propeller heads in IT will know what it is.)

Any data processing equipment—from rented PCs to mainframes—not moved from the alternate site to the recovered building should be copied or downloaded, and then scrubbed of all data so future users cannot access it.

11. Relocation to Recovered Site

If you're returning to your old location, most employees won't need help finding that. But , whether you're returning "home," or moving to a new location, you'll need to do a little bit more work to make the transition smooth. Having your employees simply show up to work at a different location sounds fairly straightforward. And in many cases, it is...simply provide them with directions, and open the doors. However, some challenges remain, as outlined in the two sections below.

12. Clear Work Backlog (Again)

Just as work almost certainly accumulated between the disaster and the start of operations at the recovery facility, work also will accumulate while your staff and operations return to your primary site, or a new one. So, as before, if that backlog needs to be cleared before new work is processed, have your staff focus on that task immediately. While adrenaline may have peaked during the crisis, productivity most likely has not. Assuming that everything truly is back to normal—in other words, the hurricane has moved on, and the floodwaters have receded—you may need to engage temporary help to accomplish this.

13. Resumption of Normal Operations

Once you are caught up, your staff can resume normal operations. In an ideal world, "back to normal" is truly seamless: your employees simply pick up where they left off. And, depending on the nature of the disaster, it may be that simple.

Otherwise, you may have to deal with some of the following issues:

1. If the original facility was destroyed and relocated, your employees may have to get used to working in a different part of town. So, as was the case in helping them acclimate to the alternate facility, you should prepare a guide to the area's amenities: local restaurants, shopping (after all, people like to run quick errands on their lunch hour), and public transportation. Even if a new building was constructed on the site of the old one, unless it is an exact duplicate, employees could benefit from a map—if not a tour—of the office. Remember, a foosball table is a nice touch after a disaster. Spring for it yourself if it's not in the budget.

2. Significant disasters may result in the loss of life. Grief counseling for employees may be necessary. Even without casualties, some members of the team may have found work elsewhere. Those who stayed may have to take on new or expanded roles with the associated need for job training. Both counseling and training may have been needed, and provided, at the alternate facility. But it also is possible that while operating in contingency mode, your employees were sufficiently distracted and focused on meeting the needs of the organization that they buried their angst for the

moment. Once things have settled down the organization will want to ensure that their needs are met. Be prepared to meet them.

Finally, bear in mind that some employees may not be ready to return to work. Depending on the nature of the event, they may need to attend to personal needs before returning to full-time work. This brings us back to the somewhat personal questions that you need to ask during the planning phase. When cataloging personnel information it might be useful to ask "Do you foresee any commitments that could delay your return to work after an unexpected event?" Some people's lives are very fragile balances among competing demands—single parents, aging parents, children with disabilities. A crisis can upset this delicate ecosystem and leave them needing some time to get things back in balance.

The chances are most people would not be able to answer such a question in advance. So prime the pumps. If it's not violating any standards or expectations of privacy (and, at the very least, let people know that answers are voluntary, not mandatory!), ask if they own rental properties or have any other obligations that might require their attention after a disaster. If so, in the aftermath of a widespread disaster they might have obligations to their tenants.

While operating in extraordinary circumstances, employees will develop a better understanding of what they will need to do once normal operations are resumed, especially if given a date for the resumption of standard processes. "What I plan to do when I get home after this disaster..." is another type note that your employees should be encouraged to jot down whenever the thought occurs to them. You might even want to start a wiki with the most creative responses. After all, there's no law against introducing a bit of humor into a tough situation to relieve the stress.

5 Exercising Your Plan

"I didn't fail the test. I just found 100 ways to do it wrong."
- *Benjamin Franklin*

A plan is an awesome start, but an untested plan is just about on par with no plan at all. You *may* be able to get away without testing on a certain software patch or upgrade. I say "may," because what's the worst thing that could happen? You bring your systems to a screeching halt. But hey, it's all in a day's work! Kidding aside, if something as (theoretically) simple as a patch install can wreak havoc, imagine what not testing a contingency plan—which is based on best guesses for anticipated needs and alternatives in the face of a mountain of unknowns—could do. Not having a BC plan is a major oversight. Not *testing* your BC plan is a grave omission.

Before I go any further, let me swap the word "test" for "exercise." Tests are something you can fail; exercise is something which makes you stronger, healthier, and more resistant to injury and illness. Business contingency plans adhere to the same principles. There is no such thing as "failing" a contingency plan test. You exercise your plan to see what works, what doesn't , and what could work better. So, semantics aside, common exercises include:

1. Call Tree Exercises
2. Structured Walk-Throughs
3. Checklist Exercises
4. Table-Top Exercises
5. Parallel Operations Exercises
6. Full Simulations

1. Call Tree Exercises

Your organization should conduct an exercise of your call tree regularly. While some aspects of a contingency plan may be so complex that exercising on an anything more than an annual basis would be onerous, call tree exercises are easy, and can be used to spread good news or celebrate success if done creatively. Further, since in large organizations people switch roles or departments frequently, quarterly call tree exercises ensure that these changes are not overlooked. Would it really be so bad for everyone to get a quarterly reminder of the overarching purpose of the organization and key priorities? I think not. Use your imagination, and you may even find that people look forward to the quarterly call trees.

2. Structured Walk-Throughs

In a structured walk-through, representatives from each department sit around a table and talk through their plans. This exercise is not designed to test the plan's granular details. Rather, it represents a first pass that allows disparate departments to uncover glaring omissions and (more importantly) conflicts between their plans. Better to have them fight it out (figuratively) in a cozy conference room, rather than (literally) while Rome is burning around them.

3. Checklist Exercises

In any complex endeavor, be it business continuity or a rocket launch, a checklist makes sure that all of the critical items are performed. The weakest printed checklist is stronger than the strongest, most experienced memory. Ideally, the person responsible for his area's plan pulls out the checklist. "Do we have paper forms on hand? Check. Is our call tree current? Check." And on it goes, down the hundreds of items on the list. Besides, no one will remember these items when up to their hips in flood waters, wading up the street with their computers held above their heads. Checklists work. Just make sure they're waterproof.

A checklist exercise also can be performed at the organizational level to confirm that there are sufficient PCs at the alternate site, for example. In summary, the purpose of the checklist exercise is to identify that key plan elements are current and available, and identify any holes in the planning process while they can still be fixed easily.

4. Tabletop Exercises

Somewhat like a ride in a NASA flight simulator, a tabletop exercise is a guided *verbal* simulation. The business contingency planning team, or independent consultant, develops a disaster scenario, and then the response to the disaster is simulated by talking through their response, following the checklists, of course.

Participants begin with the assumption of a normal workday. They get their coffee, exchange gossip, check their email...and then—simulated disaster strikes! At this point the disaster scenario is distributed, and your employees react to it. Sometimes, a tabletop exercise is a full simulation that ends at the point of relocating to the alternate facility. Have your employees take notes during and after (but especially during) a tabletop exercise. Encourage them to document response plan gaps as well as less-than-obvious details that, during a disaster, could be assets or liabilities.

5. Parallel Operations Exercises

The primary purpose of parallel operations exercises is to confirm that backup data is accessible, complete, and usable, as well as assure that alternate facilities are operational. As part of a parallel operations exercise, some employees will need to go to the alternate facility and test the equipment, using live data. Another option is to use the previous day's data, which then can be reconciled with the prior day's results. Although a parallel operations exercise is complex, it is not as unnerving as a full simulation because normal operations are not disrupted.

6. Full Simulations

A full simulation is the most complex and comprehensive form of exercise. As with the tabletop exercise, a full simulation exercises the response to a disaster scenario. But whereas the tabletop exercise stops short of transferring to the alternate site, in a full simulation your employees abandon the primary facility and resume operations at the backup location. Think of it as a field trip, only less fun. The military is fond of such operations, sometimes calling them "war games", Military personnel on call for such simulations are instructed to keep a bag of clothing and personal items packed at all times. I've heard that some people would only stuff a duffle bag full of towels and telephone books, only to be surprised when their call to "practice" turned out to be a real trip overseas.

You can add a measure of realism by having certain employees portray victims. (Make sure to have plenty of fainting written into their scripts, and some fake blood, too. Like I've said before, there's no reason this can't be exciting!) Participants should assist victims and then cope with their absence at the alternate site. Full simulations are the most challenging, but most realistic, type of exercise. And they really shine a spotlight on your plans' problem areas.

To underscore the importance of a full simulation, various United States federal agencies have conducted four such exercises, known as the TOPOFF full-scale exercises. The first TOPOFF exercise, TOPOFF 2000, was a cooperative effort by the Department of Justice, the Department of State, and the Federal Emergency Management Agency in May 2000. More than **6,500** federal, state, and local personnel engaged in a full-scale response to a multi-faceted threat that simulated a biological attack in Denver, Colorado and a chemical attack in Portsmouth, New Hampshire.[18] The Department of Homeland Security conducted three subsequent exercises, in 2003, 2005, and 2007. Considering the problems that I cited with regard to simple call trees, not surprisingly, the post-event report from TOPOFF 4 reported that most problems were in the area of communication. Specific comments included, "Participants reported delays in receiving responses to classified Requests for Information," "Decisions and taskings were not formally disseminated," and "Departments and agencies (D/As) at all levels of government lacked critical information at times."[19]

One final point worth noting: in actuality, the quotation that starts this chapter is quite appropriate. You can't fail, but your BC plan exercises *should* find 100 things you did wrong. If they don't, then like your doctor, I'm going to recommend more exercise.

---

18. TOPOFF Exercise Series Fact Sheet. Downloaded 12/22/2007 from
    http://www.globalsecurity.org/security/ops/index_topoff1.htm
19. After Action Quick Look Report. Downloaded 8/24/2010 from
    http://www.fema.gov/pdf/media/2008/t4_after%20action_report.pdf

6 | Plan Maintenance

"One must always maintain one's connection to the past and yet ceaselessly pull away from it."
- *Gaston Bachelard*

Another truism worth citing here is, "The only constant is change." Your organization will change. Your employees will change. Systems will change. Your business model might change. The world around you will change. And your business contingency plans need to change, too. Business contingency plans should be reviewed and revised, at a minimum, on a yearly basis.

In addition to the annual review, update your plans in response to events within your organization:

- **Update plans with exercise results.** It may sound obvious, but after your organization has gone to the trouble and expense of conducting an exercise, incorporate the lessons learned into your plan.

- **Update due to organizational and personnel changes.** Perhaps your company completed the acquisition of an enterprise in a different region of the country. Perhaps your organization has expanded its core business. Perhaps you have realigned your departments, downsized, rightsized, capsized, or excised a number of people. No matter what the change may be, it should be reflected in an update.

- **Update as per IT configuration changes.** If data stores have migrated from standalone servers to rack-mounted or blade servers, such a change could impact the recovery effort.

- **Update because of application changes.** New applications can add new interdependencies and affect the required recovery sequence. Conversely, valuable time and resources can be spent during a disaster recovery effort trying to recover undocumented decommissioned systems.

And most importantly, **review your plans after any event.** *Any* event. Remember, if you're a BCP professional, you're being paid to be paranoid.

7 Selling BCP to Management

"Everyone lives by selling something."
- *Robert Stevenson*

Business managers should not need to be sold on the concept of a business contingency program. (Then again, business managers shouldn't have to be sold on the benefits of long-term thinking, clear priorities, and effective communication. But that's a whole other Scrappy book.) Management should be well aware of the challenges posed by terrorism, increased government oversight and mandates, data loss, and the liability of employees with access to mission-critical data, the latter leading to ever-increasing opportunities for them to accidentally corrupt or delete this data. So business contingency planning should be an easy sell. But just in case....

The Insurance Argument

A business contingency program is a form of insurance. We pay insurance premiums to replace our homes, repair our cars, or cover our medical bills. In my lifetime, I've written many such checks. Regrettably, I have had to ask my insurer to give me some of my money back following an automobile accident. But I have never made a claim against my homeowner's policy. Yet despite the lack of a claim, I have not once said, "It sure would be nice to get something back in return for the thousands of dollars I've sent them over the years." Quite the contrary, I am relieved—even happy—that I never have asked my insurer to re-pay my "investment." Insurance is the cost of recovery from a catastrophic event.

Corporate management should take the same attitude toward business contingency programs. They are a cost of doing business...though one they probably will never have to make a claim against. But that should not weaken their resolve to invest in them!

The Process Improvement Argument

Contingency planning is a corporate necessity that may provide unexpected benefits. Beyond ensuring an organization's viability following a disaster, contingency planning can lead to operational improvements in the normal course of business.

While researching and documenting a business contingency plan, you may find hundreds of single points of failure (SPOFs). A SPOF is any single input to a process that, if missing, would leave the process or processes unable to function. SPOFs, when identified, can be eliminated—or at least have their damaging potential mitigated. Many business functions can be improved as a result of BCP efforts, particularly while exercising business resumption plans.

Many business functions must be duplicated to ensure continuing operations. Inputs to critical functions should be duplicated at the backup site should the primary input fail. This strategy is common with electronic systems, such as telephones and computers. An unanticipated benefit of installing backup systems is load sharing: the backup can be used to increase efficiency during normal operations or handle overcapacity situations.

Boring Statistics

When all else fails, fall back on the old standbys: fear, uncertainty, and doubt, commonly referred to as "FUD."

A 2006 study by Sentech examined the cost of downtime across various industries. In the health care sector, the business cost of 60 minutes of downtime was $1,593. Not surprisingly, businesses in the industrial sector fared far worse. An industrial outage of the same duration resulted in an average loss of $130,673 for enterprises in the chemicals and allied products fields.[20]

According to the Institute For Business & Home Safety, "at least one-fourth of all businesses that close because of a disaster never reopen."[21]

Below are some older statistics which, current or not, nonetheless underscore the need for adequate disaster preparation.

- Half of all organizations which experience a disaster without a business contingency plan go out of business within two years, according to IBM's Business Recovery Service Study.

- Within five years, 80 percent of companies suffering an extended disaster are out of business, according to the University of Minnesota Study of Disasters.

The bottom line is that recovering from a disaster takes time and money, two commodities that enterprises have only in limited quantities. Your job is to sell this program to the people who control the

---

20. "2006 Update of Business Downtime Costs." Sentech, Inc. Downloaded 2/9/2008 from http://bit.ly/bNB2IF
(www.sentech.org/Publications/2006%20Update%20of%20Business%20Downtime%20Costs%20Final.pdf)
21. Downloaded 2/12/2008 from http://www.ibhs.org/business_protection/

money. So think about it from your executives' perspective... in what ways (borrow from above, or create your own FUD statistics) will your BCP program help them achieve their goals, or avoid what seems completely unpalatable?

8 Selling to Employees

"Evangelism is selling a dream."
- *Guy Kawasaki*

A business contingency program must be endorsed and embraced by senior management. But to succeed, a business contingency program also needs user-community support, because it will be the end users who are tapped to provide and execute the plan's critical details.

However, you may find the average employee is hesitant to contribute due to largely unfounded fears. Employees have a variety of reasons for resisting a company-wide contingency planning effort. Three major reasons are that it takes a great deal of work, it can appear to undermine their job security, and it may seem like a futile effort to prepare for an unlikely event.

This reluctance can be overcome by imaginatively explaining how a well-developed business contingency program improves job security, how contingency planning lessons can be applied to their personal lives, and how some contingency planning activities can enhance their work experience. By doing so, you will find it is easier to get the workforce on board.

As everything I have written to this point should make clear, a successful business contingency program needs far more than data recovery strategies. It requires your employees to examine their daily routine and catalog the details of their jobs in step-by-step details. Procedures must be rationalized, documented, tested, and revised. That takes time and effort. And I would bet that a note saying, "I have too much time on my hands" *never* has been put into *any* workplace suggestion box *anywhere*.

Employees may be apprehensive about documenting the minute details of their jobs since, in theory, management could unceremoniously boot them out the door, replace them with entry-level newbies, and then use the detailed job functions for training them.

Finally, employees may see the business contingency exercise as a waste of time, since the chances of a large-scale disaster affecting them or their work location are slim.

To counter these perceptions, you must sell contingency planning both up and down the company hierarchy. Here are some strategies that have worked for me.

The Job Security Argument

The biggest challenge is fighting the "it can't happen here" attitude. Most American businesses will never face a disaster on the scale of the 9/11 attacks. But terrorist attacks are not the sole source of a business disruption. No area of the world is immune to natural disaster. Corporations in Tokyo have monsoons that stop the commuter trains from running. Businesses in Europe have volcanoes that prevent air travel. Companies in the northern US have snow. None of this is completely unexpected, but sometimes it's surprising. A storm front that causes a blizzard in Boston can affect locations as far south as Georgia. (The U.S. state, not the former Soviet State; that would be one heck of a blizzard, wouldn't it?)

Chapter 8: Selling to Employees

Your employees must understand that any event which interrupts the ability to conduct business—large or small, mundane or extraordinary—impacts the organization's bottom line, and ultimately their job security. The Boring Statistics cited previously offer some justification. Then there is the common sense argument. Even a non-catastrophic event might result in a $1 million loss. For a multi-billion-dollar company—or Bill Gates personally—that loss might be a drop in the bucket. For a smaller firm, a $1 million loss might translate into reduced benefits or a reduction in staff, and possibly deeper direct impacts to employees. In a worst-case scenario, a significant financial hit might result in the closing of the business. Your job is to convince employees that any business loss has the potential to trickle down to them.

You also should frame the detailed documentation of employee job functions as a positive exercise that could actually make their jobs easier in the long run. No matter how productive they actually are, most employees feel that they're overworked. Persuade them that cataloguing the minutiae of their daily activities—while requiring an up-front investment of time—could result in long-term workload reductions by uncovering inefficiencies, redundancies, or tasks that should be done by others.

People generally like to feel helpful, useful, and needed. Emphasize that good business contingency planning is a tangible way for employees to contribute to the success of the business. Saying "We need your help." is not some kind of "leveraging our synergies/working smarter not harder" corporate-speak. "We need your help." is the truth, and puts a human face on what some would consider an odious effort.

The Personal Enhancement Argument

The application of business contingency planning lessons to employees' personal lives is another selling point. For what is contingency planning? It is foresight and good organization. Or just a healthy (??) dose of paranoia. Make it personal. Show your colleagues how they can apply the basic tenets of business contingency planning to their daily activities, such as vacation planning—What would I do if I lost my glasses or my prescriptions?—or family emergency preparedness. The American Red Cross provides resources to help families ready themselves for emergencies. These materials are available at http://www.redcross.org. Post this URL on the company website, and encourage people to download and review the materials. Better yet, ask the local chapter of the Red Cross if it could offer a presentation about disaster preparedness to employees. Send a clear message: we care about you and your loved ones, and you should, too. Help them understand that caring about loved ones includes preparing for unlikely, but possible, events that could put them in harm's way, and practicing these plans. Other applicable websites include http://www.ready.gov, http://www.bt.cdc.gov, and http://emergency.cdc.gov/preparedness, as well as commercial outfits such as http://www.preparedness.com and http://www.quakekare.com. (I really like that last site's name, but it gives me the shakes.)

The idea is to get your employees to begin thinking like the always-terrified worry-worts that those of us who work in BCP truly are. A disaster-ready person at home makes a better disaster-ready employee.

The Work Enhancement Argument

A work-from-home program is a step that businesses can take to induce employees to create *ad hoc* off-site preparedness. Though not practical for every business—or every department within a business—letting employees work from home on a regular basis may be a beneficial long-term strategy, both from a business contingency planning and a morale perspective. Yes, it's true. After decades of resistance to allowing employees work from home businesses are finally being advised to mandate that 20 percent of a given team work from home on a scheduled basis. If that arrangement is not feasible, perhaps employees could work four 10-hour days, likewise rotating time at home. The idea is to have at 20 percent—or more—of your workforce somewhere else each day. The underlying rationale does not have to be as dramatic as thinking, "If the facility is instantly vaporized by an alien death ray, at least one-fifth of our workers will survive." The reasoning can be more mundane: if there is a gas leak or an electrical outage which slows or stops work at the primary site, at least someone can answer the phones while the rest of the team is waiting in the parking lot for the emergency to be resolved.

To illustrate, I can share a personal anecdote. On the morning of September 11, 2001, I had a doctor's appointment, and decided to work from home. Shortly after the attack, my office (a high-rise tower) was evacuated. Many of my colleagues did not shut down and undock their laptops. Instead, they (understandably) grabbed their personal effects and *ran* unceremoniously from the building. Since I had my laptop at home, I was able to continue working. Can I say that, thanks to me, we stayed in business that day? Not even in my most heroic dreams! But I was able to monitor our systems and report that everything was operating normally during several teleconferences that afternoon.

Work-at-home days also afford employees the opportunity to work while ill, both conserving their personal time off and still making useful contributions to business. Often, an employee who feels slightly under the weather will come to the office to avoid burning a sick day, possibly spreading a cold, H1N1, or whatever, to those around him. (Imagine how history would have been different had Typhoid Mary run a home-based business.) But, if working from home is an option, ailing employees will be more likely to remain at home, in their fuzzy pajamas and slippers, sipping cocoa, which will both speed their recovery and prevent them from infecting others. Likewise, during inclement weather, employees can work productively from their homes—cozy by the fireplace—rather than wasting their energies on a long white-knuckle commute. The bottom line: more people working and fewer wasted company dollars. If only we could convince managers that their employees won't just laze around pretending to work! Liberal work-from-home policies require trusting relationships and an emphasis on results produced, not hours worked. That's a cultural change that might be beyond your reach, but perhaps, in some small way, your BCP efforts can move your company in that direction.

Paint Your BCP Initiative Green

Many components of a green computing initiative dovetail nicely with business contingency planning, allowing you to prepare your organization for a calamitous event, save money, and save the planet in one fell swoop. Green is sexy, popular, and has lots of support these days. Package some of your BCP initiative in a green wrapper and see how support for your efforts increase.

- As suggested, regularly scheduled work-from-home days keep a percentage of your workforce and their equipment out of harm's way. But four-day work weeks translate into your employees reducing their work-related gasoline consumption by 20%. And though it's somewhat pie-in-the-sky, if every company established a program allowing a percentage of its workforce to "non-commute" one day per week, that reduction in traffic would ease congestion on the roads for those who are driving to work, helping them save gasoline through less stop-and-go.

- Building on the previous bullet, if an employee is not there, he's not basking in the glow of his desk lamp, feeling the breeze from his desk fan, grinding beans and brewing coffee, charging his iPod and cell phone...you get the idea.

- Building even further, fewer onsite employees mean fewer square feet of office space are needed, meaning your organization could seriously consider moving into smaller digs. (Don't laugh...this is actually being done in that bastion of all things progressive, namely, Cleveland, by a corporation in an industry known for progressive, bleeding-edge thinking, namely, banking.)

- Laptops not only are more portable than desktop PCs, but they also use less electricity. The same goes for LCD monitors when compared to the nearly extinct cathode ray tube (CRT) monitor.

- Powering down your CPU and peripherals when not in use saves energy and reduces wear and tear, in theory increasing their lifespan and time-to-failure.

- Electronically stored data is more portable (and therefore more widely available in an emergency) and eco-friendly than paper copies. But, as already stressed, make sure there are a few paper copies in case we unexpectedly enter the Dark Ages again.

- Old data centers, like old refrigerators, absolutely suck energy, much of it due to the inefficiencies of air-flow-based cooling. So if you haven't quite gotten around to replacing your data center yet, moving some of your processing power (both "peak demand" and backup) to a modern, water-cooled cloud-based facility will lower your electric bill and the region's overall carbon footprint.

Wrap Up—The BCP Department

"I am above the weakness of seeking to establish a sequence of cause and effect, between the disaster and the atrocity."
- *Edgar Allan Poe*

It is no understatement that technology has lead to 21st century enterprises enjoying quantum leaps in productivity and efficiency. But, these improvements have come at a price: we now are incredibly dependent upon our modern technical miracles. Email, fax, voicemail, and cell phones are essential for communication; PCs make each employee a knowledge worker; and servers and mainframes hold critical businesses data, the currency of the Information Age economy. Many individuals wonder aloud how they ever lived without a smart phone, with built-in GPS, instant updates of every kind, and a constant flow of email, tweets and Facebook updates to feed their connection addiction.

As reliance on technology grew, businesses developed strategies to maintain operations during various magnitudes of disaster. However they soon realized (frequently learning the hard way, or from the misfortune of others) that restoring data and equipment would not be enough to recover a business if their employees could not get to the facility, or there was no longer a facility available. Through this realization was born the discipline of business contingency planning.

Originally seen as an IT issue, business contingency planning now is regarded as an enterprise-wide effort. (At least it had better be.) A business is more than data. Business operations rely on processes. For a manufacturer, it may be that data only supports those processes, in the form of customer lists, accounts payable and receivable ledger entries, and tax-related documents. In the case of a knowledge enterprise, the data *is* the process.

These processes need people to operate them. In turn, people need a place to perform the operations and the tools to do their job. Business contingency planning is a necessary corporate function—on par with payroll and legal—which ensures that whatever the world throws at them, the people, place, and processes can continue to operate as effectively as possible.

Any small disaster can pinch a company's bottom line; an Irwin Allen production could drive it out of business. As such, a BCP department is now as essential as a payroll department. All businesses—large and small—need a well organized, well thought-out, and well-exercised BCP program.

But where to start? By picking up this book. (The latter statement is geared to those who like to read the ending first.) If you've gotten this far (now addressing those who start at the beginning.) you should now know that you will need to:

- Initiate a project to set scope and establish teams.
- Conduct an impact analysis.
- Undertake an in-depth strategic analysis.
- Establish an emergency response and operations program.
- Write the plans.
- Sell sell sell the plans.
- Test test test the plans.

Your goal, as a BCPer, is to avoid ever having to see your company's name listed in the "obits" on the front page of the business section.

Preparing for every unknown contingency is impossible. But, preparing for the unexpected *is* possible if you gather the right people, ask them the right questions, and take the right steps.

A hundred years ago companies didn't have a corporate social responsibility initiative. Fifty years ago few had a task force on making the business more eco-friendly. (Heck, back then, people smoked at their desks, and put out their cigarettes on the desks of co-workers that they didn't like!) Only relatively recently has there been a widespread need for compliance departments. Someday every serious business will have a business contingency plan, and every sizeable one will have a BCP department. What would make it possible to establish your BCP department? Perhaps it's as simple as suggesting that one is needed, and taking on the responsibility of seeing it done.

Change happens when people care enough to step up and do what's required. That person could be you, and today could be the day.

Keep it Scrappy!
- Michael

P.S. Drop me a note at scrappy@MichaelSeese.com and let me know what you've done to establish or improve your organization's BCP effort.

A BC Program Checklist

☐ Identify Assets

    ☐ Physical assets

    ☐ Information assets, such as proprietary knowledge, trade secrets, and customer lists

    ☐ Find and organize

    ☐ "Clean house"

☐ Rate System/Application/Data Criticality

    ☐ Define "critical"

    ☐ Customer-facing

    ☐ Employee support

☐ Determine System/Application/ Data Recovery Order

    ☐ Mission-critical first

    ☐ Examine dependencies

    ☐ Examine timing

    ☐ Application recovery priority survey

- [ ] Determine the "Pain" Threshold

  - [ ] Maximum allowable downtime (MAD)

  - [ ] Maximum tolerable downtime (MTD)

- [ ] Determine Existing Vulnerabilities

  - [ ] Examine current assets' vulnerabilities, the potential threats against them, and possible countermeasures

  - [ ] Fix the no-brainers

- [ ] Examine Potential Threats

  - [ ] Imagine the "dark side"

  - [ ] "Doom & gloom" session

  - [ ] Rate likelihood

  - [ ] Anything is possible; what is *probable*?

  - [ ] Rate impacts

  - [ ] Don't overlook "collateral damage"

- [ ] Evaluate Countermeasures

  - [ ] Consider built-in safeguards

  - [ ] Add low-cost safety nets

  - [ ] Review Audits

  - [ ] Look for simple, easily overlooked problems

- [ ] Focus on the Loss, Not the Event

  - [ ] It's not the disaster; it's the *consequences* of the disaster

  - [ ] Incremental responses

☐ Research and Establish Backup Storage Alternatives

    ☐ Removable media: CDs, DVDs, USB hard drives, thumb drives

    ☐ Daily vs. real-time backup

    ☐ Back up to "The Cloud"

    ☐ Secure your backups

    ☐ TEST your backups!

☐ Research and Establish Recovery Alternatives

    ☐ Hot, cold, warm sites

    ☐ Far enough to avoid the same disaster; close enough to get to

    ☐ Find local amenities

    ☐ Low-cost alternatives: unused space at your "Topeka office," vacant commercial space, other local businesses

    ☐ Plan for security at alternate site

☐ Establish Lines of Succession

    ☐ Who can "make the call?"

☐ Establish Disaster Criteria

    ☐ When does a bother become a disaster?

    ☐ Localized vs. widespread event

☐ Establish Disaster Declaration Criteria

    ☐ Can we tolerate 12 hours offline?

    ☐ Make sure you can contact the decision makers

- ☐ Establish Relationships with Local Emergency Services

    - ☐ Meet the mayor, chief of police, fire chief, and services director

    - ☐ Know how to reach them in an emergency

    - ☐ Have them warn you of disruptive events

- ☐ Develop Communications Plans

    - ☐ Think outside the phone box

    - ☐ Email blast

    - ☐ Post (privately) to the internet

    - ☐ Include suppliers, partners and customers in your communications plans

- ☐ Establish Business Contingency Plan Distribution Strategy

    - ☐ Make some paper copies

    - ☐ Keep them current

    - ☐ Keep them secure

- ☐ Establish Return-to-Normal Criteria

    - ☐ Who sends the "all clear?"

    - ☐ Define "all clear"

B BC Plan Checklist

☐ Catalog Personnel Information

    ☐ What skills & deficiencies could be significant

    ☐ Visualize the scenarios

    ☐ Don't cross the privacy line

☐ Catalog Job Functions

    ☐ "What do you *do*?"

    ☐ Ask about end-of-month and end-of-quarter

☐ Catalog Business Processes

    ☐ Explain all jobs

    ☐ Remember automated processes

    ☐ Ask probing questions

    ☐ After a crash, note how you "un-crashed"

- ☐ Draft Detailed Standard Operating Procedures
  - ☐ Who?
  - ☐ What?
  - ☐ Why?
  - ☐ Where?
  - ☐ When?
  - ☐ How?
- ☐ Catalog Equipment Requirements
  - ☐ PCs, of course.
  - ☐ Do we need printers? Scanners? Faxes?
- ☐ Develop Manual Procedures
  - ☐ Can it be done on a PC without network connectivity?
  - ☐ Can it be written down and entered later?
  - ☐ *Some* work is better than no work
- ☐ Establish Call Trees
  - ☐ Who calls whom?
  - ☐ Get multiple numbers
  - ☐ Put two lists in one hand
- ☐ Cross-Train Job Functions
  - ☐ No critical functions in the hands of only one person
  - ☐ Job shadowing
  - ☐ Schedule regular sessions

C Forms! Forms! Forms!

"Every evening, I come home tired and have just enough energy to fill out the endless tax forms."
- *Fritz Zwicky*

When developing a business contingency plan, there is a plethora of information that must be collected: Critical systems, employee contact information, vendor lists, business partner communication channels, media contacts, governmental liaisons, hardware needs, and office supplies, to name a few. Once collected, this information must be organized and stored.

A variety of vendors offer technical solutions that help organizations gather, tabulate, and report on their basic business needs. Then, if the need arises, these plans can be pulled out of a drawer, dusted to remove the cobwebs, and executed. To find such a solution, just dial up "business contingency (or continuity) management software" in your favorite browser. You will see household names like IBM and SunGard, as well as specialty firms such as Coop Systems, EverGreen and ErLogix.

Unfortunately, a smaller organization might not have the resources to purchase a commercial solution. Fortunately, most offices have the tools they need in house, in the form of the Microsoft Office suite or other Word-like applications. Word provides the front end, which enables you to create a variety of forms that can be completed by the departmental subject matter experts (SMEs). You then can create a database, using Access or other applications, to store the responses and produce any necessary reports.

Create the Form

Microsoft Word is a decent tool for the physical creation of forms, that is putting actual form elements—text boxes and check boxes—on the page. In fact, Word offers two levels of form controls.

If you never have needed to make a form, the toolbars probably are not visible by default. Here are some screen shots to help you through the process. Keep in mind that the images and actual menu options could differ based on the version of Microsoft Office you are using.

To get started, select "View/Toolbars" and choose "Forms" to activate it.

Graphic 4: MS Word/Forms Toolbar

The basic Forms toolbar gives you many of the controls you need for most forms, such as text-entry boxes and check boxes. In my experience, these controls have met most of my needs.

If you need more powerful forms, use the controls in the Control Toolbox. Select "View/Toolbars" and choose "Control Toolbox" to activate it.

Appendix C: Forms! Forms! Forms!

Graphic 5: MS Word/Control Toolbox Toolbar

These controls are ActiveX controls, which allow macros or scripts to be associated with them. In order to take full advantage of them you should know some Microsoft Visual Basic for Applications (VBA), which comes dangerously close to propeller-head knowledge. Be advised that, since these controls contain macros, your users will see a scary macro warning message when they open the form, which may prompt them to run away screaming. You'll need to counter that urge to flee in some way, perhaps by telling them, "Macros can be evil. As a rule, don't trust them. But I made these. They're not evil."

Let us assume you want to use the basic Forms controls to create a simple employee info form. Such a form probably would feature primarily text boxes, although it might include some check boxes and drop-down lists as well. Drop-down lists are especially useful for information that needs to be exact. For example, "manager's name" could be used to sort employees for a call tree. But if one employee enters "Sudhi Venkataraman" and another types in "Sudhir Venkataraman," they will not be grouped properly under the same manager in the database. A drop-down eliminates these types of discrepancies, as well as typos such as "Hunan Resources" (a tastier version of human resources, no doubt).

To insert a control, simply put the cursor where it should appear on the form, and then double-click the control's icon on the toolbar. Poof! The magic of Microsoft makes it materialize. Then add a relevant label.

A drop-down box requires you to pre-populate it with the list of choices. After inserting the control, right-click on it, and select "Properties" to display the following dialog box:

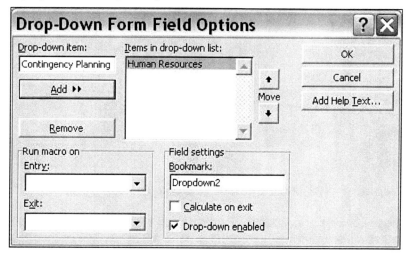

Drop-Down Form Field Options

Drop-down item:
Contingency Planning
Add ►►
Remove

Items in drop-down list:
Human Resources

Move

Run macro on
Entry:

Exit:

Field settings
Bookmark:
Dropdown2
☐ Calculate on exit
☑ Drop-down enabled

OK
Cancel
Add Help Text...

Graphic 6: MS Word/Control Properties

Type in the first drop-down item, click the "Add" button, and proceed to the next one. After entering them all, you can use the up and down arrows to the right of the list to rearrange them. Click "OK" when you're finished entering them all.

If you are using the Control Toolbox toolbar, some of the functions, such as text boxes, require you to supply a label—assuming you *want* one, though I can't imagine why you would not—as a separate element. Others, such as check boxes, have the label associated with the control.

When you double-click on the check box icon, the following element will appear on your form.

Graphic 7: MS Word/CheckBox

Right-click on it, and choose "Properties." The box below will pop up:

Graphic 8: MS Word/CheckBox Properties

You then should change the "Caption" property (highlighted in this example) to something appropriate.

Somewhere on your form you will probably want to include a date field. Aside from the obvious reason—knowing when the form was completed—it will help later when importing the information into the database. A regular text field can be formatted to accept dates. After placing the control, right-click on it and choose "Properties" as shown below.

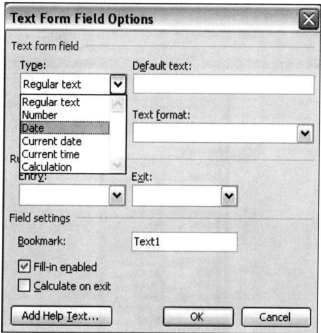

Graphic 9: MS Word/Text Field Properties

"Date" is an option in the "Type" field. You can use the "Default text" field to indicate to people filling out the form that you want them to choose a certain format (e.g., MM/DD/YYYY), and the "Text format" field to force it.

Appendix C: Forms! Forms! Forms!

After adding some elements, below is a sample of what part of your form might look like:

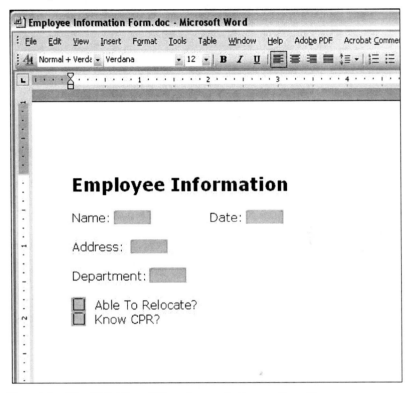

Graphic 10: MS Word/Employee Information Form

Once you have completed the form to your satisfaction, you must "lock" it, which does several things. First, it prevents uppity users from altering the layout and contents of the form itself. Second, it allows users to tab from field to field. And third, certain controls—check boxes in particular—do not work quite right in the unlocked mode.

The lock control appears on the Forms toolbar.

Graphic 11: MS Word/Form Lock

Although not necessary, you probably should make your form "read-only." There are two advantages to a read-only form. First, it prevents *you* from accidentally saving what should be a blank form with dummy data in it when filling in information during your testing. More importantly, it forces your users to save their version using a different—and hopefully relevant—name, meaning you will not be receiving a dozen different completed forms all named "Employee Information Form." After saving and exiting the document, navigate to the directory where it is stored, and right-click on the file name. When you select "Properties," the dialog box below will appear:

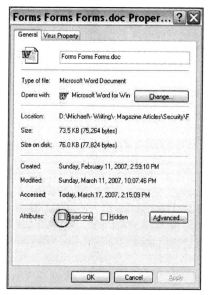

Graphic 12: MS Word/Read-Only Property

Check the "read-only" box and click "OK."

Distribute the form to your users with a deadline for completion and some kind of enticement to do so, then wait for them to filter back. Go get a coffee—you'll have time. When, inevitably, only a paltry number of forms are returned, you'll need to become more creative about how to get people to provide you their information. Holding up paychecks strikes me as incredibly motivating, but you may need to explore other options if your payroll department is one source of tardy responders.

Create the Database

The next step is to create a database with one table for each form. If using Microsoft Access, Open it and choose "File/New," select "Blank Database," and give it a clever name. (This process could vary slightly, depending on the version of Access you are using.)

NOTE: The database file's extension will be .mdb, as in BCP.mdb. When the database is open, a "lock" file with an identical name, but the extension .ldb, will appear in the same directory. (I mention this so you don't have to have the same "duh!" experience that I had when I first noticed that file.... "What is that #@#$!%* file, and where did it just go?")

The blank database will appear as below:

Graphic 13: MS Access/Blank Database

Although there is a wizard to create tables, a simple one can easily be created using the "Create table in Design view" feature. Click on this and you will see the following:

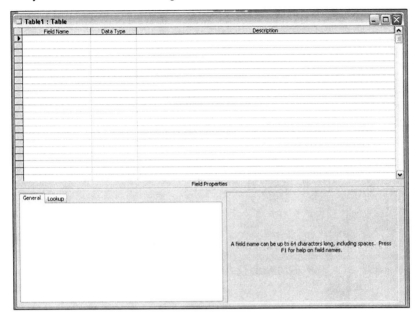

Graphic 14: MS Access/Table Design View

In the first "Field Name" row, type a name representing the *first* field in the form. It is best to not use spaces between words in the field names. For example, a good choice for the first field in this case would be "EmployeeName" (NOT "Employee Name"). Tab over the to "Data Type" field. "Text" will be the default choice. In most cases that will work just fine. Choose "Memo" for a field that will contain a lot of textual information.

Save the table by choosing "File/Save" (or using the "disk" icon) and entering a logical name. Then continue entering the remaining fields. For the date field, choose a format from the box in the lower left that matches the date format required by the form.

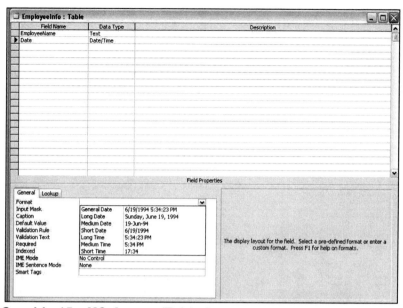

Graphic 15: MS Access/Table Design View, Date Field

For the check boxes, choose "Yes/No" as the Data Type. Once you have entered all of the fields, your table will look something like this:

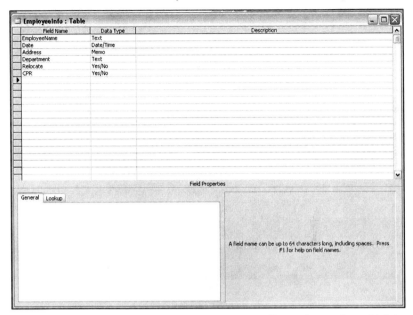

Graphic 16: MS Access/Table Design View, Complete Table

When you are finished, save the table. (If we've learned nothing else from this book, it's save your work frequently!) You will be notified that you did not create a primary key (you silly amateur). A key helps with database organization and searches by ensuring that each record has its own unique identifier. (If *you* think having two nearly identical records is confusing, just imagine what it does to a poor, non-reasoning software application.) Therefore, you will want to create a key. In most situations, the best type of key is an auto-generated number, and Access will offer to automatically create such a field. The problem is, your documents will have no such field, which will make importing more difficult (though not impossible).

A better choice is to create a key manually. A key has to be unique, but it can have multiple components. That is another reason why I suggested including a date field. A particular employee's name alone probably won't be unique, since he may create several such forms or plans over the years. And you could easily have several employees with the same name—there are more "Yuko Satos" in the world than you might think. But in most cases employee name and date together will create a unique combination. On the other hand, if one employee will be feverishly filling in multiple forms on the same day, you might have to expand the key to also include, for example, his or her department, or the plan name.

To create a multiple-field key, click in the box to the left of the Field Name (where the arrow appears to the left of the "Date" field in the previous image), hold down the CTRL key, and click in another box. Once you have selected all of the necessary fields, click on the "key" icon (circled in red, below). After you click the key, you will see the following:

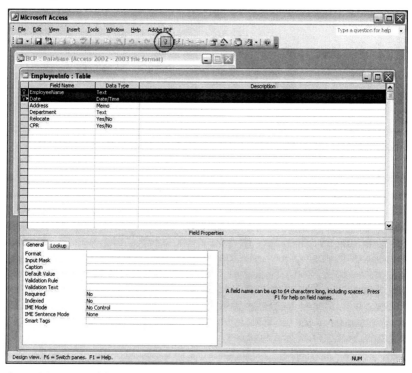

Graphic 17: MS Access/Table Design View, Create Key Fields

Your table now is complete. Close it, and you will see it added, as shown below:

Graphic 18: MS Access/One Table Completed

Create any additional tables you will need. Your database is now finally ready for data. Of course, by now you may have had a disaster strike, and there you were—just about ready to upload the disaster preparation information. Oh well. Type faster next time!

Enter Data

Once you have a completed form, you need to enter the data into the database. The first step is to save the data contained in the form to a text file. Open the document, and choose "Tools/Options." On the "Save" tab, click on the check box for "Save data only for forms."

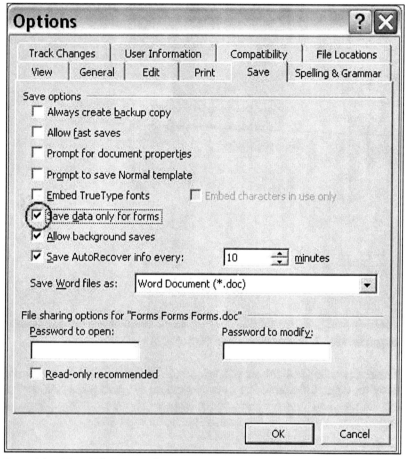

Graphic 19: MS Word/Save Data Only For Forms

Then, save the data by selecting "File/Save Copy As..." By default, it will keep the same name, but will save it as a text file.

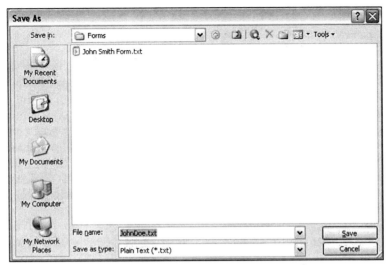

Graphic 20: MS Word/Save As Text File

Depending on the version of Word, you may get a file conversion warning:

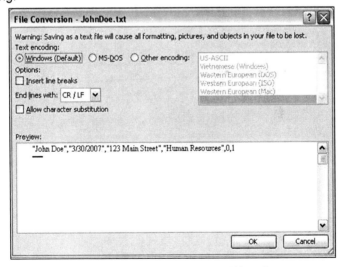

Graphic 21: MS Word/File Conversion Warning

In spite of such warnings, click "OK." You now have what is known as a comma-separated (or comma-delineated) text file.

Please note that when saving an Excel spreadsheet as text, your file also will be converted to a comma-separated format, although in this case the extension will be .csv.

It might seem sensible to check the "Save data only for forms" box before sending it to the users, since you will have to open this dialog box and check it for every form you receive. Don't go there! If you do, when your users save their documents, the default will be a .txt file. Though *you* ultimately will want it as a .txt file, your users would have to know that, and send the right file to you. More likely, they will send back the Word doc (since that's what you sent them), but it will be blank. To avoid confusing them (let's be honest, your "BCP Basics" lecture already confused them enough), you are probably better off handling it yourself.

Once you have a form saved as a text file, importing it is fairly easy.

The database must be *open*, but the table itself must be *closed*. Choose "File/Get External Data" and select "Import..." You will see the following dialog box, which by default, looks in the database's home directory:

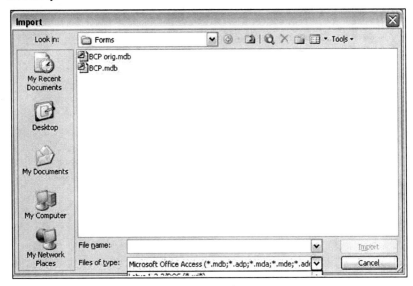

Graphic 22: MS Access/Data Import, Step 1

Use the "Files of type" drop-down box and scroll down a bit to get to "Text Files (*.txt; *.csv; *.tab; *.asc)." Choose the proper file, and click on "Import." You will see a dialog box like this:

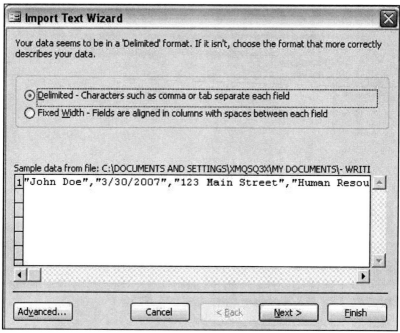

Graphic 23: MS Access/Data Import, Step 2

Because we saved the Word doc as a comma-separated text file, the default, "Delimited," is the correct choice. Click "Next >" to see:

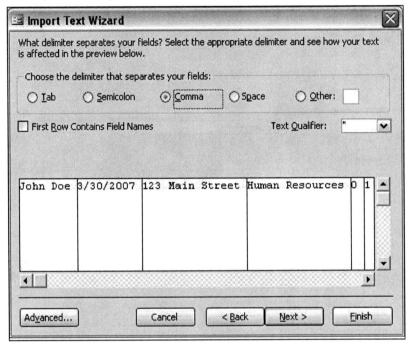

Graphic 24: MS Access/Data Import, Step 3

If "Comma" is not selected, select it. Click "Next >" once more to see the following:

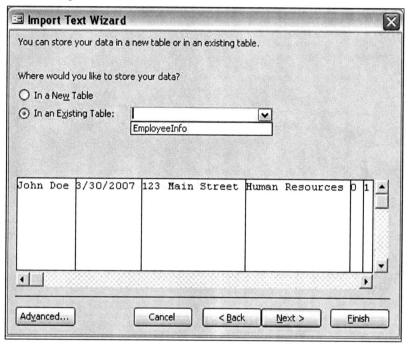

Graphic 25: MS Access/Data Import, Step 4

When you click on the "In an Existing Table:" drop-down box, you will see a list of all of the tables in this database. In this case, of course, there is only one. Click "Next >" one more time (though in most cases, you can just click "Finish" here) to see the following:

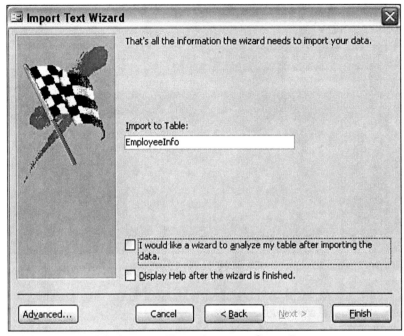

Graphic 26: MS Access/Data Import, Step 5

Now click "Finish." Assuming there were no problems, you will see a confirmation dialog box. Click "OK" to close it. If there were errors, the dialog box will report that. Bad records will be imported into a newly created table called "Paste Errors." You can sort through these afterwards.

Once you have successfully imported the first record, you will see it in your database:

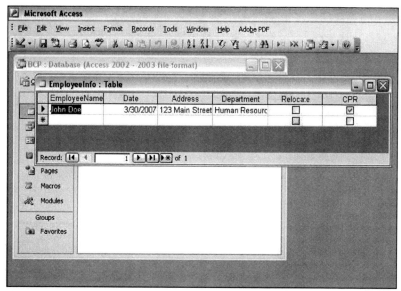

Graphic 27: MS Access/One Database Record

Now it's just a matter of collecting additional forms and entering the data in to the proper tables.

Once you are finished you will have a structured record of your organization's business contingency planning needs. You can open any table and sort the records (temporarily or permanently) to organize the records in any fashion you choose, such as by department, or even by people who know CPR. Yay!

As you work with Access, you can use the Queries, Forms, and Reports to manipulate the data to suit your needs. But we'll leave that to your future quest for knowledge. For now, be aware that all of these fancy-schmancy tools are created from the same menu as the table was, as shown here:

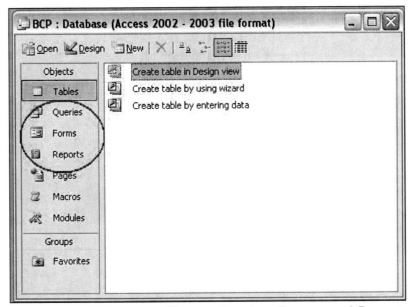

Graphic 28: MS Access/Create Queries, Forms, and Reports

The Forms and Reports are especially powerful, as they will allow your database to provide you with the kind of categorized information those expensive third-party solutions offer. But, clever you, you were able to create a solid repository of information using the techniques presented in this appendix at a fraction of the cost. Make sure your executive sponsor and your manager know THAT when it's time for your next performance appraisal!

About the Author

Michael Seese, CISSP, CIPP, is an information security, privacy, and business contingency professional in beautiful Chagrin Falls, Ohio. He holds a Master of Science in information security, which was earned completely online via a very cool synchronous and interactive curriculum, and a Master of Arts in psychology, which tends to scare people. He began his career as a journalist, and then moved into technical writing, which piqued an interest in programming, which after all is nothing more than another form of writing, using a more limited and concise language. Then one day, standing in a local bookstore and surrounded on three sides by programming books, covering C++ and C-sharp and .NET and ASP, he had an epiphany: programming languages come and go. Guess wrong—that is, specialize in the flavor-of-the-last-month—and some college fresh-out will take your job, and probably do it better. But the need to store data and protect data will remain and, in fact, grow. That realization led to his current career track.

Michael regularly speaks at conferences, has had numerous articles published in professional journals, and contributed two chapters to the *2008 PSI Handbook Of Business Security*. He is the co-author of *Haunting Valley*, a compilation of ghost stories from the Chagrin Valley. Michael also penned (or, better said, e-penned) this book's companion tome, *Scrappy Information Security*. He currently spends his limited spare time rasslin' with three young'uns, and can be reached between matches at scrappy@MichaelSeese.com.

Other Happy About Books

The Ten Commandments for Effective Standards

This book is standard reading for anyone pursuing knowledge, excellence, and success in the field of technical standards.

Hardcover: $29.95
Paperback $19.95
eBook $14.95

The Successful Introvert

The purpose of this book is to present strategies used by successful people —including numerous celebrities—in managing their introversion or shyness while becoming successful in professional endeavors.

Paperback:$19.95
eBook: $14.95

Scrappy Women in Business

This refreshingly honest book provides welcome reassurance for every businesswoman who's ever wondered, "Is it me, or has the whole rest of the company gone nuts?!"

Paperback $19.95
eBook $14.95

#PROJECT MANAGEMENT tweet Book01

This book is a handy little companion that brings you tweet-sized yet powerful insights into project management.

Paperback $19.95
eBook $14.95

Purchase these books at Happy About
http://happyabout.info
or at other online and physical bookstores.

Breinigsville, PA USA
23 November 2010
249923BV00005B/5/P